TURNING AROUND TURNAROUND SCHOOLS

2nd Edition

What to Do When Conventional Wisdom and Best Practice Aren't Enough

D1265137

FRANK DESENSI | ROBERT KNIGHT | JOE DESENSI

SILVER TREE
PUBLISHING

Turning Around Turnaround Schools:
What to Do When Conventional Wisdom and Best Practice Aren't Enough
2nd Edition

Copyright 2018 by Frank DeSensi, Dr. Robert Knight, and Dr. Joe DeSensi

Published by Silver Tree Publishing, a division of
Silver Tree Communications, LLC (Kenosha, WI).
www.SilverTreeCommunications.com

Editing by:
Susan Draus
Bob Johnson
Hilary Jastram
Kate Colbert

Cover design and interior graphics by:
Iam Bennett

Typesetting by:
Courtney Hudson

Second edition, May 2018

ISBN: 978-1-948238-02-1

Library of Congress Control Number: 2018944113

Created in the United States of America

DEDICATION

To the hundreds of educators with whom we have been so privileged to work during the past 20 years. We thank you for your confidence and your collaboration. Entire communities are stronger because of the inspiring and tireless work you do each day.

TABLE OF CONTENTS

PREFACE

DEVELOPING A NEW PERSPECTIVE FOR EDUCATION REFORM

We are a team of educators from Educational Directions, LLC (Ed Directions), an educational consulting company providing training and leadership support for K–12 schools, and we wrote this book for educators. Frank DeSensi established Ed Directions in 1998 to enable a group of retiring educators to continue to work with schools struggling to improve student learning and performance. Since its establishment, the company has worked with both urban and rural schools in several states, providing leadership development, assisting struggling schools, and collaborating with districts in developing programs and software to enhance school improvement.

WHAT'S NEW IN THIS EDITION

The first edition of Turning Around Turnaround Schools was well received, but some readers asked for more concrete examples and tools to implement the ideas in the book. In the second edition, we have expanded several ideas about "student as learner" versus "student as performer," added samples and use cases for capturing and using the right data, and developed tools for most chapters to jump-start the real-world implementation of these ideas.

HOW WE GOT HERE: A QUICK REVIEW OF SCHOOL REFORM

Modern reform started around 1895, the beginning of the first national movement to change education. Since that time, education has undergone reform about every 12 years.

Before this most current period of reform, educators tended to plan using what is now called the education model. Educators identified problems in student performance by testing failures or patterns in disaggregated scores and then reformed some element of textbooks, teacher training, methodologies, or school schedules. Teacher evaluations focused on the implementation of the reform initiatives, and success or failure was determined by the teacher buy-in and use rather than student achievement.

Modern reform started around 1895, the beginning of the first national movement to change education. Since that time, education has undergone reform about every 12 years.

The latest national reform movement produced the No Child Left Behind (NCLB) Act. This movement dated back to about 1990 and changed the focus of instruction from teacher compliance to student performance. NCLB is a standards-based reform with high levels of accountability for improving student performance. It required educators to make data-driven plans that enabled each student to use what he or she has learned at the levels defined by a standard and, as a result, necessitated an approach to data management and planning that was not a part of teacher education programs in colleges and universities or teacher professional-development sessions in states and school districts. It also required academic leadership — rather than merely school and classroom management — from teachers and administrators.

HIGH-STAKES ACCOUNTABILITY AND THE ORIGINS OF THE TURNAROUND MOVEMENT

The stakes for educators in Kentucky changed dramatically in 1990 with the passage of the Kentucky Education Reform Act (KERA); this was a response to the state Supreme Court's ruling stating the previous funding formula for Kentucky schools was unconstitutional. The legislature, executive branch, and a coalition of interest groups formed a consensus around a comprehensive package of measures that reached far beyond how schools were funded in the state; they created a completely new approach to schooling and school management — an approach in which schools and districts would be held accountable for their students' performance as measured by a standards-based assessment.

Suddenly, the state was keeping score (something educators were not used to). It took several years for educators to fully understand the impact that decision would have. At the time of implementation, several of us on the Educational Directions senior team worked at the state level to help implement the change toward standards-based education and to support schools that were struggling with student performance. In this role, we had the opportunity to observe the problems schools faced when using traditional methodologies to change student performance and schools' difficulties in dealing with institutional mandates that got in the way of them doing what they needed to do to improve learning and performance.

We set up Ed Directions to enable a group of early standards-based innovators and practitioners to continue to work with schools and districts after retirement. As a new company, we used distinguished educator strategies as the basis for our turnaround work. Over time, our methodology evolved as we learned more about student learning, thinking, and performing; today, our company has reached a point where we feel we can turn around a school if we get access to it in a timely fashion and the school and central office support the approach that we advocate. It is important to note Ed Directions does not market a product but develops an approach to teaching, learning, and data management that is appropriate for a high-stakes accountability world.

We set up Ed Directions to enable a group of early standards-based innovators and practitioners to continue to work with schools and districts after retirement.

The genesis arose during a "What's next?" discussion among members of the Ed Directions leadership team. As we tried to develop a strategy for a particularly difficult school situation, we reflected on how our approach to assisting schools and our best practices have changed since 1998. Initially, our thinking was that this would be an internal document we would share with newly hired coaches during onboarding. When it became clear what we were outlining was going to be more substantial than a white paper, we decided to develop a book.

Our initial effort at outlining a book produced enough material for three or four books. Cutting material was as difficult as writing it. In the end, we focused on how our approach to changing student performance changed from the 1990s to the present day. It's important to note that in most cases, we did not rush willingly into change. The changes we describe in this book required us to give up ideas and strategies we knew were best practice and had been used with some success. We needed and searched for new solutions. This proved to be more difficult than we expected.

We also include a description of how the schools reacted (especially the institutional elements within schools) to our attempts to take them out of their comfort zone. Marketing some of the changes we were trying to get schools to implement became as important and as difficult as developing the tools and strategies to produce the changes.

Since the first edition of this book, more states have moved to high-stakes accountability for schools with a scorecard that, in many cases, involved state testing as one of the metrics of success. We found that many school districts are more open to our approach of creating an entirely new educational system; in this system, the learner is the most important piece, and educators use baseline and tracking data to see if interventions are showing progress for students in their dual roles of learner and performer.

Since the first edition of this book, more states have moved to high-stakes accountability for schools with a scorecard that, in many cases, involved state testing as one of the metrics of success.

We hope you, the reader, approach this book reflectively. As you see how our thinking has changed, we want you to challenge your own preconceptions. This is not to say you must replace your game plan with ours, but you must own your own plan. This book is not the magic bullet or the only answer. We think of it as a beginning. There was never a single solution to turning schools around — the answer changes as the students change, the teachers and administrators change, or the scorecard for success changes. This book is more about describing a process than defining a canned plan or one-size-fits-all program.

We hope that reading this book will help you become a better selector and consumer of programs and that you will base your metrics of success on how student performance is positively impacted.

A NOTE FOR FULL DISCLOSURE

This book is intended for those who work in or with turnaround schools, though the approach to education presented works with any type of school (public, private, charter, and so on) at any level (struggling, passing, blue ribbon, and so on). We hope to share the lessons we have learned and describe strategies and processes that have proven successful for us. Most importantly, we hope to provide for you a set of understandings and tools that will guide your work and make you a more intentional, effective agent of change.

It is also important to note we come from the world of the practitioner instead of the world of the researcher. We do strive to be well read and informed, and in the acknowledgments section, we cite numerous people who have helped shape our thinking through their work; however, the unique insights we have gained in the past 20 plus years have been shaped more by our direct work with students and educators, and for their sake, we hope you read it.

PRACTITIONER'S NOTE

At the end of the introduction, Ed Directions has provided a self-assessment tool that you can use to assess your school or district. If you are a practitioner, we recommend completing the assessment before reading the book and again upon finishing the book to see if your perspective of your school or district has changed.

At the end of each chapter are tool kits that Ed Directions developed to address some of the issues described in that chapter. The other tools are data sets the coaches in Ed Directions find invaluable to making sure they are data-driven in their approaches to intervention and progress can be tracked throughout a school year.

INTRODUCTION

DEVELOPING A NEW PERSPECTIVE FOR EDUCATION REFORM

Most Ed Directions staff started this work as administrators in struggling schools, and several were selected by the Kentucky Department of Education to work in support of low-performing schools in the mid-1990s.

Unique to Kentucky's education reform legislation at the time was a provision calling for the development of a cohort of distinguished educators (DEs), who were charged with assisting (and sometimes taking over and running) schools and districts that were identified as being in decline or crisis (as defined by the Department Education). This team was formed with little or no specific plan of action. No user's manual for improving school results existed anywhere at that time.

As leaders in struggling schools and later as distinguished educators, we became confident we understood the education reform process. We studied the latest theories on thinking work, rigor in the classroom, behavior rituals and routines and so on. We knew how to disaggregate data, triangulate data, and link data to school plans.

In the mid-1990s, we started to change our work. We abandoned our concept of best practices that we were taught — a set of common preconceived notions about how schools could improve. At the risk of oversimplifying, we were sure that if the curriculum aligned with what was tested and if the teachers taught it well enough, the students would score better on the next high-stakes test.

Sure enough, alignments revealed significant gaps in the curriculum of many schools, and students' low scores on parts of the test usually mirrored these gaps. This combination of curriculum alignment and test disaggregate, along with teacher training, the use of accepted best practices, strategic planning, and heightened supervision of teachers, became the go-to approach to school improvement in those early days. As a result, many schools showed gains in test scores.

In the mid-1990s, we started to change our work. We abandoned our concept of best practices that we were taught — a set of common preconceived notions about how schools could improve.

However, this approach of focusing on inputs — teachers, curricula, and testing — to drive improvement wasn't enough to move the more challenging and persistently low-performing schools and students. Even when these schools dutifully went along with making the necessary input adjustments, the students still struggled to make gains on the high-stakes assessments. While input work may have produced tangible or intangible improvements in some schools, test scores too often remained stubbornly flat, achievement performance gaps widened, and schools continued to underperform. Eventually, we realized we needed some way to identify the priority problems. We had to find and face research that addressed and preferably offered solutions to those problems.

THE MOVE FROM INPUTS TO OUTPUTS

When we got into the business of trying to change student scores instead of trying to improve the adults, we had to come to grips with several new realities; we started on a journey that was full of potholes, roadblocks, and wrong turns. We found that turning a school around was more than just implementing programs. It involved an intentional, relevant data approach to improving students in classrooms.

When we got into the business of trying to change student scores instead of trying to improve the adults, we had to come to grips with several new realities; we started on a journey that was full of potholes, roadblocks, and wrong turns.

Wrestling with this disconnect between intervention and results produced the first of a series of "aha" moments, which helped us move our thinking from the input side (the adult side) to the output (the student) side of the equation. Chief among them was the realization that *input change* produced *accidental results* if it did not meet the priority learning needs of the students who were actually in a given classroom. If we did not focus first on the needs of those students, it was impossible to get the results that we wanted, because only those students would be doing the learning and, ultimately, taking the test.

The needs in underperforming schools were numerous and systemic. It was easy to identify many of the critical needs, but that in itself was a problem, as trying to fix too many things at once diffused efforts and taxed limited resources, such as time and money. Getting schools to look beyond adult priorities and focus first on the needs of the students as learners and performers required a major change in our and their thinking. Not having an aligned curriculum is not as detrimental to student performance as having 80 percent of your students unable to read the questions on the state assessment. We shifted our focus from priorities that had no or little bearing on test scores to those that had a direct impact on scores because, like it or not, test scores were the ultimate metric by which we were being judged. Struggling schools must improve as learning institutions, but districts or state departments of education must see tangible results in a single year. To ignore test scores is to possibly doom a decent plan that might take several years to show systemic results. Band-Aids and quick assessments of the most fixable issues do not get a school to a long-term, systemic fix as an organization, but they can give it some breathing room by helping it show some immediate results.

The development of our approach to turnaround schools didn't come in one wondrous insight. Rather, it developed in many steps and in leaps and bounds as we came to grips with old realities that were no longer relevant.

In chapters 1 through 6, we describe how we recognized problems in our old realities, reexamined our thinking, and developed new strategies focused on student priorities. These new strategies, techniques, and tools became the nuts and bolts of our approach to working with schools. However, we found we did not have the luxury of turning them into magic bullets. As new data came in from schools, we adapted and modified. Eventually, we accepted the fact there was no one approach we could use. Rather, we assessed each school as an individual case. This simple change in educational focus and approach allowed us to help schools address their unique problems and develop individual plans for improving student work and student performance.

Chapter 1 explores our first struggle with a foundational piece of the education world as we knew it. In the old reality, test scores provided all the information we needed to plan and lead. We would disaggregate, triangulate, set goals, and make plans that were driven by the test scores. In some states, all school plans had to reference state test scores. The first change in our methodology as a consulting company was to address the inadequacies of test scores as decision points. Today, we still use test scores, but we use them to raise red flags in areas that need further study. We made test scores a starting point, not a decision point.

Chapter 2 focuses on our second struggle with the realities of our old world: proficiency. The state required proficiency, but nobody could define what it meant in terms of student performance. We knew the students had to know the content, but we also identified students who knew the content but did poorly on tests. We found there was more to a student being proficient than content knowledge. There were, in fact, a wide range of characteristics and competencies that students required to be proficient.

Chapter 3 looks at what happened when state departments of education added successful transition expectations for students; we found that teachers had to look beyond just the competencies required for test proficiency. There were several other competencies that were required for transitions to a new grade level or to the world beyond high school. These new competencies had to be addressed in both the top and experienced curriculum offered in the school.

Chapter 4 addresses the issue of causation and root-cause analysis. Once we could define what schools had to produce in their proficient student, the process of determining why students were not proficient became more complex. Originally, we assumed if they missed questions, they did not know the content. However, that assumption was no longer viable. Eventually, we developed a process for looking at the student work and identifying the point of breakdown. The process then focused on determining why it broke down at that particular point. This established the cause of breakdown and enabled us to become more effective in designing student work and support systems for underperforming students.

Chapter 5 explores the problem of progress monitoring. As DEs and early on in our consulting work, the majority of schools with which we worked were required to use some type of data management system. However, most focused on disaggregating and triangulating some type of test scores. Schools could provide a linear record of student scores by groups, but many times, they used the scores to identify and provide appropriate programs and strategies for low-performing demographics or problematic groups. One of our tasks was to get schools to treat students as individuals and monitor performance for both learning and test taking.

Chapter 6 examines the issue of school planning and how planning needs to change for the standards-based world. It examines two sample plans — one that approaches a problem from the input side (the adult side) and another that approaches the same problem from the output side (the student side). The plans are compared to show the way the focus affected the goal setting, development and monitoring elements of the plans and how the expected outcomes of the plans were different.

Chapter 7 focuses on our efforts to assist schools in redefining best practice. Early on, schools and districts tend to select, purchase, and implement nationally marketed best-practice programs and materials in the hope that they will raise scores. As we worked with schools, we found the programs' materials were rarely best practice for every student. In some cases, instead of scores improving, they went down. We came to understand if the strategy or material did not match the needs of the students, it was not best practice for those students. Getting schools to identify who their students were and what the students were required to do made it possible for the schools to develop an intentional plan for moving all their students to the levels expected on tests or for successful transitions. For us, best practices are those practices that intentionally improve individual student performance. We judge their efficacy not by how they change the teachers' teaching but by how they change the student as learner and performer and his or her work for the better.

Chapter 8 examines a process that Ed Directions developed to track student progress when scores provide an imperfect data set. One of the accomplishments of Ed Directions in school turnaround efforts was the development of a new type of data collection system, the Academic Review (AR). An AR enables us to establish a baseline for teaching and learning practice in a school and then to revisit the school at the end of the year to identify how that baseline set of teaching and learning behaviors has changed. This enables us to identify positive changes in a school when the changes haven't yet translated into significantly higher test scores.

ORTHODOXY'S BACKLASH

These core practices allowed us to help persistently underperforming schools focus on a more manageable and targeted set of changes. By focusing on the student and his or her work as the problems to fix, we discovered that we could defuse an unfair blame game that sometimes develops in tough schools.

Coincidentally, the student focus also brought us face to face with a whole new set of issues endemic to turnaround work — issues rooted in the cultures of some schools and districts. Endeavoring to shift turnaround work to the output side, to a student-performance focus, we encountered surprising backlash from several sources that made this work far more problematic than necessary. We address some of these issues in the last three chapters of the book.

We found that these cultural issues are rooted in a sort of orthodoxy of belief and practice that envelops some schools and school systems. We use the term orthodoxy because it best encapsulates the rules, roles, and relationships that drive life in these cultures, and many of them stand squarely in the way of turning schools around. We discuss a few of them in the following chapters.

Chapter 9 recounts one of our major problems in going into a school as a change organization: that we have to deal with adult issues and not just student issues. We find that many times stakeholders value turf over performance, and we find ourselves involved in fights over what defines best practice in a discipline (for example language versus direct instruction in reading or skills development versus concept mastery in mathematics). Many times, we are forced to fight about whose job it is, who has the last say, whose materials are used, or, most importantly, whose fault it is. Another adult issue that frequently has to be addressed concerns the role you play when faced with change. Staff members of every school or district play a variety of positive or negative roles. Change agents need to know what those roles are and how to deal with people who are playing a role that is negative toward our change efforts.

Chapter 10 recounts an opportunity to lead a state-mandated turnaround effort in a large district. In short, we were granted control of the academic program in seven schools and empowered with the authority to address these issues head-on. These schools were firmly rooted in a compliance-oriented, input-dominated culture. None of the schools that we worked with were truly "broken schools." Rather, most were underperforming because they were not addressing the learning or performing needs of students. We discuss how these schools worked to become more autonomous and intentional learning communities. We present the test score results attained at year-end and offer a debrief on the effort.

Chapter 11 summarizes our conclusions about our approach to education but acknowledges that our process continues to evolve. The federal government and individual states are still changing the education game and the school-to-work initiative is going to add more competencies to a list that already exceeds most school's ability to manage output expectations. We hope that our student-focused approach will make the transition to any changes made in the next generation of changes. If we keep the student as the focus and we move the students toward whatever expectations are established, *we can improve student performance.*

SELF-ASSESSMENTS AND TOOL KITS

There are tools at the end of each chapter. The first edition of the book referred to *helpful data* and targeted data collection tools. Some readers asked for more specifics and examples. As a result, we included some of the tools Ed Directions developed and currently uses in working with struggling schools. In some cases, they collect baseline data, and in other cases, you will note ongoing tracking data sets to monitor intervention impact and success. You do not have to use these exact tools; you can take ideas from how we applied the information in this book into real-world data sets.

PRACTITIONER'S NOTE

This book is set up to challenge some of the thinking and approaches that educators utilize to improve schools. We have included a self-study that can serve as a pre-self-analysis or post-self-analysis for educators. We encourage you to work through the self-study before you read the rest the book.

INITIAL SCHOOL SELF-STUDY

1. **Check each of the items that you can learn from your state assessment report:**

   ☐ Areas where the school curriculum is strong

   ☐ Areas where the school curriculum is weak

   ☐ Students who are performing proficiently

   ☐ Students who do not know content

   ☐ Priority areas in need of strategic planning

   ☐ Areas where professional development for teachers is needed

2. **Check the items that you can learn about students from test scores:**

   ☐ Students who cannot read

   ☐ Students who cannot perform mathematical computation

   ☐ Students who cannot write proficiently

   ☐ Students who need remediation in science, social studies, reading, or math

3. **Identify all the data points that you use in your school or district to determine which students are proficient:**

   ☐ State test scores

   ☐ District benchmark or interim test scores

   ☐ Teacher-made test scores

   ☐ Teacher evaluations

   ☐ Scores from nationally normed tests

4. **Check the items that your school or district uses as primary tools in planning:**

   ☐ State test reports/state rankings

   ☐ District benchmark and interim assessments

   ☐ Whole-class diagnostic assessments

   ☐ Teacher preferences for professional development

5. **Which of the following data points does your school or district use to determine the professional-development program for teachers?**

   ☐ Teacher suggestion or preference

   ☐ Administrator suggestion or preference

   ☐ Recommendations from central-office curriculum or content specialists

   ☐ Suggestions generated from attendance at conferences or symposia

   ☐ Suggestions generated by new technology, materials, or programs purchased by the district

01

THE HIGH-STAKES TESTING CONUNDRUM

Educators devote their lives to a profound purpose: educating the next generation. Education is the greatest gift and provides the best foundation on which to build our society. With finite resources, such as time and funding, administrators look for help and solutions to the problems they face in turnaround schools.

At Ed Directions, our cumulative experience taught us that the most common error in the approach to helping struggling schools comes from trying to force-fit a one-size-fits-all solution or from just tweaking a component of the school rather than looking at it holistically. In the mid-1990s, we as a group of educators got tired of pretending that schools were getting better and decided to actually help them get better. In part, this meant accepting the premise that most of the theories and best practices regarding helping turnaround schools were flawed or, at least, incomplete. The approach defined in this book is not one program that can fix all schools but, rather, one process by which to identify root problems and implement a unique and interactive action plan.

This turnaround in turnaround thinking means being
student-focused in both operational planning and curriculum
design, asking the right questions to inform planning, knowing how
to interpret the available data resources, monitoring progress, and,
in most cases, navigating politics. Sometimes when you look at the
whole process at once, it seems insurmountable. Although reforming
schools is no small task, it is manageable. Use the tools this book
offers. Learn from our experiences. Implement suggested changes.
Above all, realize you are the expert in your school. No one has the
firsthand knowledge you do. It takes time and intentional design to
improve student performance, but it can be done.

---

*This turnaround in turnaround thinking means being
student-focused in both operational planning and curriculum
design, asking the right questions to inform planning, knowing
how to interpret the available data resources, monitoring
progress, and, in most cases, navigating politics.*

The first step on our journey from school reform experts to effective turnaround agents was understanding the limitations of one
of our most fundamental realities: state test result reports. Most of
the Ed Directions senior staff was involved in school reform before
it was required by the state of Kentucky in 1991. As school administrators in the 1980s and 1990s, we were introduced to the practice of data mining. We learned to disaggregate and analyze test
scores and demographic data and use this analysis to drive decision
making in our planning for the next year. We thought we were effective consumers of data, and as long as no one was accountable for
student performance, we were correct. Some of us were so good

at using data that we were selected to be Kentucky Distinguished Educators (DEs).

In the Distinguished Educators program, we found the new Kentucky school accountability reports contained different types of data. Quickly, we got involved in disaggregating, and slicing, and dicing the different data silos. We asked schools to spend enormous amounts of time using our data references and triangulating data from different sources to create data charts; we developed complex plans for improving test scores. Scores were our foundation. Our problem was many times the plans we developed did not work.

As the emphasis on high-stakes testing increased, the accompanying school accountability placed a tremendous amount of pressure on schools. These test scores became the elephant in the room no school planning team could ignore. The mountains of statistical and analytical reports generated from the state test reports, combined with the mountains of data schools could get from other sources, encouraged schools to disaggregate by race, gender, socioeconomic status, and so on. It was seen as a great opportunity. We could make a plan for almost any group.

As the emphasis on high-stakes testing increased, the accompanying school accountability placed a tremendous amount of pressure on schools.

What we did not understand at the time was that we couldn't trust our test scores. This whole approach was based on a set of assumptions that we soon learned were more often false than true:

- We assumed test scores accurately measured students' knowledge of the content. Low scores were presumed to mean the student did not know the content.

- To use the test scores, we assumed that most students gave their best effort on every question on the tests, beginning to end. Less than best effort would give a false read of what the students knew.

- We assumed all students had mastered the various question formats used on the tests. If they did not know how to answer some of the types of questions included on the test, their scores were a false read of what they actually knew.

- We had to assume they could fully read and understand the test questions and they were prepared to think at the levels required on the assessment. If they lacked critical reading and critical thinking, they could know the content and still miss the question.

- We assumed scores from one type of test (for example, multiple choice) were as valuable as scores from another type of assessment (for example, open-response questions or performance events). Tests were tests, we thought, and the results could be used interchangeably. If they gave us different types of data, which ones could we use?

- We assumed all test scores were valid and that test scores from the previous year's standardized testing cycle could be used to identify this year's priorities. The argument that we are grading schools and not students on state tests assumes that the strengths and weaknesses established in one year's level of performance could be used to plan for the next year.

This conventional wisdom led us to conclude test scores held the key to identifying any school's priority needs. In thinking this way, turnaround leaders like us required schools to spend many hours of their planning and professional discussion time looking at patterns in test scores and deciding what the adults needed to do differently. We sought specific, test-score-tailored, research-based best practices to implement in our classrooms.

Early in this new era of school reform, a data-focused testing approach benefitted most schools. Focusing on the test and the specific content included on the test had a positive impact on class-rooms, and in many instances, scores did, indeed, rise. However, most of the lowest-performing schools stayed low performing. We found in these schools, this high-level and cursory use of student test data was just as likely to give us a false read as a true one. We found plans built on false reads would yield accidental or haphazard plans in terms of meeting the real needs of the actual students in a class at a particular time. We found accidental plans sometimes produced positive results but not always the ones we expected. Sometimes those plans had no impact on student performance, and in some cases (more than we like to think about), they caused the situation to get worse. We decided we should change the data and the way we use data to generate plans so the plans would be current and intentional for the students present in class. Three cases, in particular, demon-strated how our perception of reality changed.

AHA MOMENT #1

The first issue that caused us to rethink our approach to using test scores to drive change occurred in a school where we were asked to provide assistance after the start of the school year. Our first task, we thought, was to look at the school plan so that we would have some frame of reference to use in our discussions with teachers.

We noted the planning team for the school had already developed several remedial programs in reading, writing, math, social studies, and science. When we talked to administrators and teachers about these programs to see how they were checking on implementation and impact, we found the programs were not being implemented. When we asked, "why not?", we were told most of the students they'd identified as candidates for remediation were no longer in the building. When we probed further, we found that indeed some of the students had moved to different schools (the school had a very high mobility rate), but others had simply been promoted from the middle school to high school. When we asked about current students who might need remediation, we found the school had no idea which students were not performing proficiently in the different tested areas. They collected no performance work to check their current students against the expectations and were surprised that we expected them to identify the students and get them involved in remediation as quickly as possible.

As a result of these continuing discussions, we found the previous year's results were descriptors of last year's students. In reality, none of those students, even if they were still in the building, were the same students who had been tested last year. Some moved, others were promoted, and all of them were older and more mature than the previous year.

In this case, we immediately started collecting current data on students and updated the school plans for support and monitoring of student performance. When we figured out using last year's scores to dictate plans for this year's students was an imperfect way to support student performance, we began developing plans relevant to the students who would be tested this year. But, perhaps more importantly, this *aha* moment acted as a catalyst for us to question other assumptions about test scores.

AHA MOMENT #2

During the early years of our company, we worked with several middle schools. Their data indicated social studies students were consistently scoring low in the US Constitution portion of the test. All of these schools had labeled this as an area of priority need, and they had included in their plans several curriculum and professional development (PD) initiatives to address that specific problem. A few schools even decided to spend considerable money on a more engaging and interactive program.

A year of implementation passed while the new curricula and methods were employed. However, when the data came back from that year's test, even though each school reported that the units on the Constitution were tremendously successful, there was barely any improvement in student performance. Students were more engaged, and even teachers enjoyed the lively lessons and support that the program provided. But, why hadn't the scores improved? The students were obviously taught well, and their classwork showed they had learned and mastered the content.

Deeper probing of the data raised a few red flags. When looking at results from previous years, we noted the students usually scored high on the multiple-choice parts of the test — high enough to infer they knew a great deal of the content being tested. However, they were scoring very low on the constructed responses — the written portions of the test.

It just so happened, each year, the test had one long, scaffolded, constructed-response question on the Constitution. We interviewed students and discovered many would blow off this constructed-response question, answering only a part of the question or not answering it at all. The students gave several reasons for this, but mostly, they hadn't seen that type of question before and didn't have the desire to invest the time and energy on written responses.

This was a transformative moment in the evolution of our approach. The schools accurately identified an area of concern. They took a commonsense step to the conclusion that they needed to do a better job of teaching a weak area; then they developed good plans to correct the teaching. We had no doubt the content of the curriculum improved, and the adults became better deliverers of content; however, they were *already* doing well at teaching the content, as evidenced by the relatively high multiple-choice scores. The real cause of the low subdomain score was performance on one type of question — constructed-response — and in probing the students, we discovered a large number of them struggled with those types of questions in all content areas. In many cases, the struggle was related to the fact that they had never been asked to respond to complex questions as a part of their regular schoolwork. They had no experience answering questions that included three, four, or five thinking steps, and none had experience with written responses that demonstrated that thinking to a reader.

The schools initially framed the problem in terms of assumptions. School leaders assumed lower test scores were the result of inadequate content knowledge. They developed plans to fix the problem, but the plans did not work. When the school leadership probed deeper for more specific causes of the low scores, they uncovered serious student performance issues around one type of question. Sure enough, when they continued probing, they found the problem fundamental to this type of test question not only affected social studies test scores but *all* subject test scores where these types of questions were used. This new problem, when effectively addressed, had the potential to leverage results across the board, not just in social studies.

Afterward, we were pleased to see improvement plans focused on written-response performance resulted in higher test scores for these otherwise-stagnant schools. Not only did their overall scores improve, but with teachers embedding such questions into their ongoing classwork, students' critical thinking and written expression skills increased exponentially as well. The complex thinking required by such questions amplified the rigor of student work in many class-rooms. We found it helps to solve the right problem.

AHA MOMENT #3

Another revelation came at a school where it appeared that very few students understood science. In the process of probing beyond raw scores, we again found something that forced us to drastically change our approach to analyzing test scores. In this school, we helped the school leadership team probe into patterns of responses and samples of student written responses. We found in almost 60 percent of the students who appeared to be less than proficient, some variable other than content knowledge was the major issue.

Simple disaggregation of the data did not adequately explain why student performance was low. However, when we looked closely at each student's performance on the test and compared performance to the teacher's estimated performance, we found some interesting patterns. In the following chart, we included three sample students from this examination of 120 different student response patterns. In all three cases, the multiple-choice response indicated a low level of content knowledge about science.

Table 1 Answer Sheet

Question #	Correct Answer	Student 1	Student 2	Student 3
1	D	A	D	D
2	B	B	B	B
3	A	C	A	A
4	A	A	A	B
5	B	B	B	C
6	C	C	D	D
7	D	A	A	B
8	B	B	C	B
9	B	C	D	A
10	A	A	A	C
11	C	B	B	D
12	D	C	C	C
13	C	A	B	B
14	B	B	C	A
15	A	C	B	C
16	C	A	D	C

Student 1 only got six questions correct. His science teacher noted that he was not very involved in the education process, so this was an excellent score for him. Student 2, in contrast, scored lower than the teacher expected. He was a good student and motivated to be perfect when tested but he was also very insecure and test anxious. He was bothered by distractions and had a hard time getting back on task after interruptions. Student 3's marks were a shock to everyone; he was a straight-A student who planned to go to medical school. He had attained the highest science grade in the school for three years running and had completed more science credits than any other student in school, yet, he failed to exhibit a high level of content knowledge.

These students — different in socioeconomic status, program placement, and academic performance — all scored in the same range. The school, true to its remediation plan, placed all three in science remediation. After all, didn't the data indicate all of them needed it? (Some of us did question why students had been placed in science remediation when those students would not be tested in science in the current year.)

As we analyzed the work of Student 1, it became obvious he used the Christmas tree pattern to fill in his answers: A, B, C, A, B, C. His score was a false read because his performance was unrelated to his actual knowledge.

After checking the student records, teachers discovered the student had passed no classes in his high school career and regularly gave no effort during the lessons. He missed 22 days of school and was tardy to science class 11 times. In this case, we had no idea whether or not the student knew any science, but we were sure his attitude was a problem. We were also sure science remediation was not the intervention he needed most. Troublingly, when asked about current students who had similar profiles, the staff had no idea how students were grouped beyond raw scores. A review of their records showed many other low-performing students shared this profile.

In the case of the second student whose data we probed, when asked what happened, he responded that he was disappointed and said he had spent a lot of time on one question and then had run out of time and guessed on the rest. The teacher remembered several disturbances had occurred during the test and testing obviously made this student anxious. Again, we uncovered a false read of student knowledge and performance level, and again, we determined science remediation would not solve the problem. When we asked about other students in this year's science class with similar test anxiety and attention issues, again, the school did not know.

In one school that was an AP center, we found that a number of advanced students scored at the novice level. The teachers immediately told us that this was because there were "other" types of giftedness that had to be included in the program. When we sat down with them and went through each individual score, we found that none of the "other" students were novice. All of the novices were academically gifted students who, as it turned out, decided the test wasn't important to them and refused to try. Further investigation proved that this attitude was introduced and supported by two of their AP teachers.

We had no idea what happened to Student 3 until someone figured out that he knew the correct answers but marked them out of sequence on his answer sheet. When he was shown his work and questioned about his performance, he was surprised but didn't seem disappointed. When asked about why he didn't catch his mistake, he said, "Nobody told me to check my work." Here, a cavalier attitude about the test, inadequate experience, and poor test-strategy preparation seemed the major issues. Science remediation was, yet again, an inappropriate intervention for this student — he probably could have taught the class. His score, like the other two students', was a false read of his knowledge and performance level. When asked how many other gifted students had taken little interest in the test or how many had poor test-taking strategies and had scored below their potential, the school had no idea.

Because of this deeper inquiry, we found several patterns that could better inform planning. Attitude about the test, time management, format facility, and testing confidence all emerged as school-wide issues that were every bit as problematic as the curriculum itself or how much science the students knew or didn't know. For the school, this aha moment led to a new and very different planning cycle.

It required a great deal of soul searching and pushback, but we came to understand that we couldn't use test scores the way we were using test scores. Using the gross scores or simple disaggregation by race or socioeconomic status did not give us the data we needed. We did discover that there were some things that we could learn from analyzing test reports. One of the most important of these was how to analyze the scores to identify red-flag issues. By looking closely at reports to detect patterns, scores, or cells that were either well above or well below our expectations, we could pinpoint areas needing more evaluation and probing. The test score was a starting point in our exploration, but we had to figure out what the scores meant before we could identify the root problem and build intentional plans to address it. With limited time, we cannot afford to waste any on the wrong problems. Fixing something quickly is no substitute for fixing the right thing well.

AHA MOMENT #4 — AGE OF DATA

Implications

Eventually, a new reality evolved to guide our work. The conventional wisdom with which we started had included data practices and premises that could not support the type or level of planning needed to turn around schools. Our new reality included several different assumptions:

- **The test report scores are outdated data points.** Most of the schools were analyzing and planning using at least six-month-old data, and the old data was mostly unrelated to the students whose scores we had to improve. To plan for teaching and learning this year, we needed data on the students in class this year. We found the more current the data sets, the more they could be used to inform planning.

- **The test scores did not provide answers by themselves.** In the 1990s and early 2000s, most schools planned from the raw scores in their school report and were guessing about causal factors rather than making informed decisions. When we started looking at all the different layers within the school test report, we found out more and more about student performance. This data mining of the scores raised questions or red flags, and we realized that the study of these is far more important and valuable for planning than any obvious trends in numbers. Mining the red-flag areas can produce a better picture of real student performance and comes closer to informing decisions than the use of raw scores. However, these still will not get us to the root cause of why a student's work breaks down.

- **The test scores don't tell us what happened, much less why it happened.** Test scores don't identify the cause even if they claim to, and they can tempt us to use labels or score numbers as though they were root causes when they aren't. Many schools are still lured into support programs for groups of students who have the same score or fall into the same demographic group. Again, this is guesswork not intentional planning.

- **Many times, the test scores can't be trusted.** It took a long time to come to grips with the fact test scores don't tell us what the student knows, what was wrong with student performance, or what went wrong with the student as he or she performed. As long as we examine test scores with the assumption they are a perfect and accurate representation of what the student knows, they can mislead rather than inform.

- **Test scores can tell you where you *aren't*, but they can't tell you where you *are*.** Test scores represent an accumulation of points by students referenced to a numerically generated cut score. They don't tell us any more than how many points a student earned or how many students in a school earned more points than the established cutoff score for proficiency. As a true indicator of performance, test scores must be a starting point for data collection, not an ending point and certainly not a decision point.

After struggling with these issues surrounding test data for 20 years, we understand that test-score analysis is necessary but insufficient to develop a true turnaround plan.

After struggling with these issues surrounding test data for 20 years, we understand that *test-score analysis is necessary but insufficient to develop a true turnaround plan.* Still, the data sets are important. It's your starting data point but cannot be your decision point. We found that the more archaic and fossilized the data and the more distance from current student-performance status, the more likely one will be to guess and hope in interventions rather than to plan intentionally. We also realized there are many other data streams needing to be monitored and linked to test performance data before we can develop an intentional, student-focused plan for improvement. We now encourage schools to do the following:

- **Data mine test scores to identify the red-flag areas** and identify areas needing more study and perhaps data generation (rather than just data disaggregation) to get to a point where we can understand what the test scores mean for planning.

- **Check test scores** against current data to see if patterns are still valid. Some schools use data that's almost two years old to make plans for this year's students. One of our group likened this to using data on a fossil bed to try to save the fossils. Schools have to check to see if the red flags are reflected in current data.

- **Build data rooms** where teachers can store samples of student learning and performing work and use those to drive professional

learning community (PLC) discussions about student
improvement.

- **Monitor both learning and performance** — on at least a weekly
  basis — to identify problems before they have a chance to perma-
  nently impact student performance.

- **Use PLC discussions to continually monitor student performance** and to probe for cause and develop intentional
  ad hoc plans.

- **Develop multiunit and multiple-year portfolios of student
  learning** and performing work to provide a linear record of
  growth and issues that limit growth.

We also came to understand that one cannot hope to change school
scores unless students change them. If we want the students to
change, then we have to collect real-time test and relevant data on all
students and use this to drive the planning process. The high-stakes,
standards-based assessments we work with today are tests of student
output, not adult output. Using test scores to change what teachers
do, which materials they use, or which strategies they implement in
the classroom is guessing not planning. It works only if the changes
match the needs of the students in class at the time. If we want to
change the output, we must change the people who produce the
output. In this case, they are the students.

For Ed Directions, this relatively simple change of perspective
shook our understanding of education. Our team struggled with the
notion we could not completely trust and develop plans solely using
test scores. Moving from test data reports to collections of data on
students as learners and performers was a giant step for us, but it

proved to be the stimulus that led to a daisy chain of changes in our perspectives and our mode of operation.

DATA, BUREAUCRACIES, AND LOW-PERFORMING SCHOOLS

It's important to note that the people who made decisions in schools did not immediately embrace this change in our perspective with open arms. While we became more comfortable looking for data beyond test scores to drive our plans, many school leaders were reluctant to give up requiring schools to plan based on the state test scores. In many states and districts, the school improvement planning process became more and more comprehensive over time, linking to the multiple funding sources subsidizing turnaround efforts. Districts and states had to account for how money was spent and measure the effects in terms of increased school test scores. This may be a good thing for bureaucrats, but it proved a big problem for schools under the accountability spotlight. School improvement plans are now as thick as phonebooks and, like phonebooks, are likely to be opened only when someone needs to look something up.

This all seems rational. Once everyone knows the plan, it is easy to build a monitoring system checking for compliance and quality of implementation. A dutiful school leader can manage implementation, hold people accountable, and report to his or her superiors that school reform is progressing well. District support staff can see how they need to align their services. Supervisors in the line of authority can measure performance quantifiably and hold people responsible for results. In short, they are planning to better manage the adults. There is one problem with all of this, though. The students, not the adults, take the tests.

In low-performing schools, plans need to focus on answering these questions: What do the *students* have to do differently? How does *their* work have to change in the classroom? How will *they* summon more effort and seriousness of purpose?

While it is necessary for schools to comply with any mandated improvement plans, these efforts are rare enough to drive a significant increase in test scores in low-performing schools. With this understanding, turnaround schools should identify a smaller set of specific causal factors from which to develop their plan-within-a-plan, which will be able to leverage a more direct increase in scores for that school. Let's call the plan of their own making the *real plan*. Three major issues make this real planning a necessity:

- Schools are awash in data sets — principals are drowning in them, in fact. Every funding source has its data-specific justifications; every external initiative needs its own data set accumulated, and educational leaders keep testing, so educators can monitor student progress. However, unless the school has student-current performance data sets that identify, assess, and address student need, it is impossible to measure progress toward more proficient learning and performing. That's what the real plan needs to be about.

- Low-performing schools have an overabundance of acute needs. Leadership's key problem in these institutions is managing the preponderance of need that exists and creating a sense of urgency around a narrow and attainable set of goals. To make this happen, the real plan is indispensable.

- Schools, especially underperforming schools under pressure to improve, can confuse the tail and the dog. The dog in the classroom is the student learning and performance. Schedules, materials, PD, and curriculum are all tails. To plan without focusing on the needs of the actual students in the classrooms (if they are there to become proficient learners and performers) is to focus on the tail and not the dog. Focusing on adult preferences or glitzy programs presented at a conference lets the tail wag the dog, and any impact on student learning and performance will be accidental whether positive or negative.

In Kentucky, there is a folk saying (paraphrased): "If you are going to take a journey, (to plan effectively) you need to know where you are, where you're going, and who's going with you." When we create a plan using only test scores, we do not really know where we are. We really only know where we *weren't* last year or the year before. To make an intentional plan that will enable us to move the students we have in class today, we need to use a data management system that provides us with current data on our students and their performance relative to the expectations of the district and state assessments. Understanding this was the beginning of our transformation from turnaround school consultants to instructional leaders.

BEGINNING A RED-FLAG ANALYSIS

In one school, the teachers based the year's plan on the assumption that the students in the biology track (advanced program, honors program, primarily Caucasian) would do better on the science exam than the students who were in one of the other science tracks offered. When we asked them to participate in a red-flag analysis, we started by looking at the demographic groups in the school to see if there was any difference. We noted that there wasn't a significant performance gap between or among any of the demographic groups.

Table 2

Group	Distinguished	Proficient	Apprentice	Novice
White	0%	5%	45%	50%
African American	0%	1%	38%	61%
Hispanic	NA	NA	NA	NA
ESL	NA	NA	NA	NA

As a follow-up, we asked about the programs and their science tracks. When we analyzed the results, we found the students were scoring well below their potential in the advanced and honor programs. Nobody knew why, so the next step was to probe the scores to find out what was going on.

Table 3

Program	Distinguished	Proficient	Apprentice	Novice
Advanced Program	0%	7%	50%	43%
Honors Program	0%	2%	45%	53%
"Regular Program"	NA	2%	30%	68%
Special Ed	0%	1%	26%	33%

Further analysis showed that the programs the AP and honors students followed from sixth grade through the tested grade completed no earth science, no physics, and very little chemistry. The sixth through ninth grade curricula focused on getting students ready for biology and passing the end-of-year biology test. We also found that a great many of the teachers of advanced and honors programs downplayed the value of the statewide testing and told the students that it didn't really count. It's interesting to note that the teachers did not know that the school had zero distinguished students on the state test, nor did they know who the proficient, apprentice, and novice students were. We were ready to start.

PRACTITIONER'S NOTE

To encourage schools to use their test scores as a starting point and not a decision point, we included in the tool kit for chapter 1: a *Red-Flag Analysis set*, a *Doing the Math worksheet*, and a *Test Format Mastery checklist*.

RED-FLAG ANALYSIS

Red flag analysis for previous year's testing results:

- Are there any areas with scores less than 50 percent?

- Are there any areas that were targeted in plans but showed no growth?

- Are there any drops in score?

- Are there any flat-line scores — basically the same score for three years?

- Are there any performance gaps between/among grade levels or teachers?

- Are there any performance gaps between/among programs? Where are they? Which subjects/grades are affected?

- Are there content areas that seem problematic? Which ones?

- Are there students whose performance declined? How many? Why did it decline?

Force rank and annotate concerns and red flags:

Concern / Red Flag	Why Is This a Top Priority?
#1	
#2	
#3	
#4	
#5	

Define action items from concerns:

Action Item	Start	End	Person in Charge	Evaluation Activities

Did we meet or exceed our academic grade goal for the previous year? If yes:

- Where did we do well?

- Were there any surprises?

- Were there any disappointments?

- Did we maintain or exceed all of the previous year's scores?

- Were there any scores below 50 percent? What do we need to do to improve these areas?

- Were there students who exceeded or failed to meet expectations? How many? Why did this happen?

- Have we set goals for 2012? Have we identified the students we must move?

- Are there any changes in students, personnel, or programs that could cause problems this year?

- Are there issue areas that we still need to address?

- Do we have plans for these areas? Have all teachers and departments/grade levels translated those plans into personal action plans?

Force rank and annotate concerns and red flags:

Concern / Red Flag	Why Is This a Top Priority?
#1	
#2	
#3	
#4	
#5	

Define action items from concerns:

Action Item	Start	End	Person in Charge	Evaluation Activities

Did we meet or exceed our academic grade goal for the previous year? If yes:

- Where did we fail to meet expectations?

- Were there any surprises?

- Were there any scores below 50 percent?

- Do we have plans for areas where we missed expectations? Drops in score? Flat-line scores?

- Have all teachers and departments/grade levels translated those plans into personal action plans?

- Have there been any changes that might improve or lower scores (students, staff, or programs)?

- Did any students fail to meet expectations? How many? Why did this happen?

- Have we set goals for 2012? *Have we identified the students we must move*?

- Have we assessed current performance levels? Are they better or worse than last year?

- Have we done the math on the new state progress monitoring process?

- Do we have profiles for the students we must move this year?

- Have we planned our data points to monitor student growth (or lack of growth)?

- Do we know what score we have to reach?

Force rank and annotate concerns and red flags:

Concern / Red Flag	Why Is This a Top Priority?
#1	
#2	
#3	
#4	
#5	

Define action items from concerns:

Action Item	Start	End	Person in Charge	Evaluation Activities

Doing the Math with Current Students

Grade: Subject: Goal: # of Proficient
                                              Students Needed:

Data Points to Be Used in Monitoring

Students' Projected Score Groups

Proficient	Not Quite	Long Way to Go	Unknown Quantity
High Performing	Almost Proficient	Almost Apprentice	
Barely Proficient	Apprentice / Barely Apprentice		

Test Format Mastery Summary Sheet

Date: Teacher: Subject: Observer:

Student	Multiple Choice	Short Answer	Extended Response	Word Problem	On-Demand Writing	Real-World Application	Response to Data

Notes:

_____

_____

_____

_____

_____

_____

_____

_____

_____

_____

_____

_____

_____

_____

_____

_____

_____

_____

_____

_____

_____

_____

_____

_____

_____

_____

_____

02

PROFICIENCY: COMING TO GRIPS WITH THE FIVE-LEGGED MODEL

It took some time to convince us that test data in and of itself was a poor indicator of what students knew or could do and that planning solely from the state report was less than best practice. It's relevant to the old Kentucky saying, "We knew we didn't know where we were, but we found out that we also didn't have any idea of where we were going." Once we accepted we did not know what we thought we knew about test data and that tests didn't tell us what we thought they told us, we had to go back to the drawing board with some of our theories about our understanding of what proficiency entails.

Most of us, at one time or another, were curriculum specialists and so grew comfortable thinking that the students who scored less than proficient didn't know the content well enough. It initially made sense to us to examine the standards and the state test specifications. By doing so, we thought we knew everything that should be included in a school curriculum. Then we would work with schools with backward design to develop curricula. In this process, we helped schools look at the content the students had to cover and develop units covering those things.

Once the focus of school improvement shifted to improving student performance on the high-stakes assessments, we found we needed to know more about what was expected of students. From state documents, we knew that students were expected to score at a "proficient" level on the state assessment and that they were supposed to make successful transitions to the next level either in or beyond school. As we proceeded with our work, it soon became apparent that merely covering the content (and even teaching it more effectively) often left students far short of proficiency. We needed to do the following:

- Better understand what students had to do with learning to be proficient

- Develop at least an initial understanding of what core elements enabled students to be proficient

---

Once the focus of school improvement shifted to improving student performance on the high-stakes assessments, we found we needed to know more about what was expected of students.

As curriculum specialists, we thought this would be a simple task. Initially, we asked the state's Department of Education testing gurus what *proficiency* meant. They defined *proficiency* in terms of the total number of points a student earned relative to a mathematically determined collection of points *that would be determined* to be the cut score for proficiency for this year. Sometimes this was done after the test as a part of a norming process, which made it very difficult for the state guru to explain to some of us how that fit with standards and expectations.

One of our group noted that if we accepted this as our driving definition, all we had to do was tweak our program enough to shake more points out of the test tree, and it didn't matter if we used Band-Aids or systemic changes. This was problematic for those of us in the school-turnaround field who wanted to help schools produce better and more proficient (in real terms) students, but it made our program marketable.

As we helped teachers focus on what was expected of students in the state standards, we ran into a major roadblock. Their perceptions of what the standards required students to do was anything but standard. Teachers in a school addressing the same standard frequently taught with different vocabularies, used different tasks and created different levels of student tests. None of them were consistent with the expectations of the unpacked standards.

In Ed Directions, we believed that if we did not get a handle on the proficiency issue, we could never define where we were going or where we were trying to get the students to go. We could never identify the data needed to determine where we were because we didn't have a reference point to use to place students on the continuum that led to proficiency.

The conventional wisdom, which we brought into the turnaround effort, emphasized using some model of backward planning or retrofitting to make sure lessons focused on the ultimate standards. While schools concentrated on student mastery of content defined as being exposed to the content elements of standards in classes, they could align their curricula to make sure every lesson had a standards reference. Backward planning and standards-based lessons dominated schools' professional-development efforts. Classes posted the standard being taught and used research-based practices to produce mastery learning.

Our problem was that all these terms were buzzwords that had little relationship to reality. The following became clear to us:

- Planning under these conditions remained *accidental* and lacked the strategic and tactical elements needed to generate a real turnaround plan.

- Unit and lesson plans were developed with a focus on the teachers' work or the content they would cover. They did not focus on what the students were learning and what they were learning to do with what they learned.

- What was covered from each standard differed from teacher to teacher and grade level to grade level. The critical language and work included in lessons were often nonstandard among teachers in the same school.

- Critical areas of content, question types found on the assessment, and a method of monitoring for learning and performing were frequently missing or misused in the classroom.

- Progress monitoring was almost always tied to student scores on tests.

- Conventional teacher monitoring could tell us when something was taught but not which students learned it or when.

- Students were provided with accidental work in terms of where they were in the learning process, their learning needs, and their performance expectations. Rigor, duration, and engagement were regular topics of discussion, but there was little understanding of the terms by the teachers and no understanding by the students.

Part of the problem was that the test documents and reports provided no information about what proficiency meant beyond references to cut scores and content or to performance summaries. There was no real way to tell what qualitative metrics were used to label one student "proficient" and another a "novice" beyond the total points accumulated by each student. The difference in scores did not explain how the work was different, where student work broke down, or why the student had missed a particular question.

There was no real way to tell what qualitative metrics were used to label one student "proficient" and another a "novice" beyond the total points accumulated by each student.

Our assistance team experienced an *aha* moment in a discussion with a school staff member about what that person thought made students proficient or nonproficient. We found many teachers didn't really know about cut scores and how students received labels. Many didn't know about weighted questions or levels of engagement. Even today, when we work with schools, we start by checking their understanding of what proficiency means and how students earn proficiency on their state report. If their understanding is incomplete or incorrect, we begin our intervention there.

As we discussed the state test reports with school staff, we found many educators never looked for patterns in their results. They looked at cumulative scores and developed their plans. Again, there was little probing to identify patterns or outliers that might help them make informed decisions about what to do next.

Probing further, we found that at all grade levels and in all departments, individual teachers had different perceptions of the standards required of them. In other words, they had nonstandard understandings of standards. This made PLC discussions inefficient and frustrating. Schools struggled to find what they had to do to raise their scores and get rid of the turnaround label, a daunting task given the imprecise understanding of what was being required of them and their students.

We found that schools responded to this problem in different ways. Some tried to deal with the situation by using their test scores to identify content problems and create a plan to fix them. In most cases, this involved getting the teachers to change either by using different materials or by following a different strategy. Some purchased a magic bullet curriculum from a vendor who marketed it as aligned to the standards. Some sought a cure-all professional-development program to encourage teachers to teach more about thinking, problem solving, or authentic writing. Most relied on Band-Aid strategies to get them to the next round of testing so their magic bullets could take effect, or so they hoped.

CHANGING THE PARADIGM: GETTING TO THE STUDENT FACTOR

Schools were spending their resources to move away from some issue and process in their past performance. In this mode, they played catch-up and solved the wrong problems. Few schools tried to make meaning of the standards expectations and develop a picture of what a proficient student looked like. Without a common understanding of the expectations, schools struggled to raise scores.

Our team members decided that if we continued to use this approach, we were doomed. We felt that while test scores could tell us where we weren't, they couldn't tell us where we needed to be. With schools held accountable for producing proficient student performance, the first challenge was defining proficiency in a way that could provide direction for leaders and teachers as they tried to adapt to state requirements.

Most schools unpacked the standards, and the leadership teams thought they were in good shape in terms of curriculum alignment. We had to convince them otherwise. We insisted that effective academic leadership started with developing a clear picture of where the students needed to be and then establishing clearly defined priorities for getting them there. Because there was little or no translation of proficiency beyond the identification of content, we decided to focus first on defining the proficient performer in content terms.

To get school attention on student expectations, we facilitated a different version of unpacking the materials that defined expectations. These included standards documents, test specifications, and samples. Dealing with multiple state artifacts required school leaders and teachers to look beyond just the concept clusters and big headings included in the state standards statements. Eventually, we focused the discussion on what the students needed to know, what they needed to do with what they know, and the level at which they needed to do it. Emphasizing the need for schools to determine what a student needed to know and what they could do, as well as the level at which the student needed to work, proved to be an attention-getter. This approach to unpacking identified the content base students needed to be proficient in terms of the accountability test, the task expectations connected with that content, and the level at which the students were required to perform to earn enough points on the state test to be considered proficient. From this unpacking process, we were able to generate the following:

- **Concept Vocabulary**

  The language of a state standard was the starting point in this effort. Each standard proved to be an umbrella statement including a large working vocabulary. Many times, this vocabulary was specific to the standards document and other parallel vocabularies that existed in the various disciplines. Regardless, this vocabulary would frame the questions on the assessment. Identifying the specific vocabulary was key. For example, in one instance, students on an end-of-year algebra test did not understand that constructing a mirrored image and drawing the reflected image meant the same thing. Because they did not realize that they knew how to answer the question, most skipped it. The first task in our unpacking activity was to develop a list of the critical concepts using the terms or language included in each standard. When expressions were ambiguous, for example, "solve an equation" or "elements of a short story," we had to try to find out how the standard or the language would be tested and then reach some kind of departmental consensus on how it should be addressed.

- **Task Vocabulary**

  If you use a paper-and-pencil test to measure student performance, it is critical that both teachers and students understand the nature of the tasks on the assessment. The task vocabulary includes the types of questions, the different venues that might appear on the test, the key words of the tasks, and the nature and level of the thinking required in answering questions. We found many students knew the conceptual vocabulary part of the content but could not identify or perform the processes or tasks that were required on the test. One problem was getting departments to develop their in-school testing program so that the in-school tests were consistent with state expectations for performance (language, task, venue, level of engagement, and format).

- **Level of Engagement**

The level at which the students engage in an activity or test question is an important issue, and includes matters like difficulty, complexity, length and duration, structure, and familiarity. For example, addition is addition, but addition in a second-grade class is different in level from addition in a calculus class. Many times, schools opt to use off-level materials, low-level assessments, and simplified, alternative vocabularies. When this happens, the schools can successfully teach students but at the expense of preparing them to perform at the wrong level, therefore, causing students to appear less proficient than they really are (or causing students to actually be less proficient).

After some years of working with schools, we came to understand that the language issue was more pervasive than we anticipated. State standards, the core content, and accountability assessments are all written in formal register, that is, they are written in the language of the discipline being tested as interpreted by the state agencies and the test riders. The expectation of the assessments is that the student will read, think, and communicate using the language of the discipline. When a student has a wide range of life experiences and a great deal of familiarity with formal language, this is not a big issue. However, for students who do not have this background or are new to English, this particular language barrier is hugely problematic. Their lack of familiarity with formal language can make it very difficult for them to demonstrate their potential as performers on a formal assessment.

In schools where dialect registers are nonstandard and more informal and colloquial, teachers themselves can exacerbate the problem. When students regularly use off-level materials and when nonstandard language and references are used and accepted in the classroom, students may not be able to succeed within the formal language of the assessments even when they know the content. For instance, students may have a general notion of supporting a conclusion with reasons and evidence, but if they are accustomed to responding to the prompt "Tell me why," they may not be able to demonstrate their thinking and understanding at the level of proficiency that the assessments expect. Likewise, classroom directions to "Show their work" may not prepare them for assessment instructions that ask them, specifically, to list the steps they went through to reach their answer.

As we shift to testing situations where short-answer and open-response questions will be more prevalent, students with language deficits will be at greater risk. When we factor in the electronic scoring of short-answer and open-response questions, we exacerbate the problem. If the classroom culture does not embrace the languages of the discipline and the test, students are not fully prepared to meet standards-based assessments.

In our first attempts to follow through with this, we spent large amounts of time helping schools do the following:

- Unpack and align their curricula and teaching materials to unpacked standards. We spent our time making sure students were taught critical vocabulary and task learnings that would be required on the test before the test was administered. In the beginning, this was sufficient to earn a bump in test scores. The time spent on the standards made teachers more clearly aware not just of the standards themselves but also of the ways learning would be defined by those standards.

- Because most of the tests we worked with included weighted items, we tried to help schools use the test specifications to develop a test bank of easy, average, and difficult practice questions. They could then use these sample questions to give students experience in answering the different types (and levels) of questions that they would face on the accountability tests.

Both of these strategies — identifying learning expectations and developing sample questions — were used schoolwide to address accountability and state test expectations. They produced results in the following environments: schools where the strategies, materials, and languages were not congruent to the standards (alignment is not enough), schools where tested content was not covered ahead of time, and schools where the students lacked experience dealing with different types and levels of test questions. In other schools where these specific problems were not the major issues, it was more diffi-cult to create improvement.

For Ed Directions, this was a problematic situation. We needed quality plans designed to improve teaching and learning if we wanted the turnaround effort to have a lasting effect. As it pertains to the folk wisdom we cited, we did not believe that schools could make quality plans without precisely identifying their end goals for students (where they're going), establishing their current status in terms of those goals (where they are), developing action plans to move all students to where they needed to be by assessment time, and monitoring the implementation and impact on learning, performance, and test scores.

Because we were hired to improve test scores, we could not ignore the imperative to raise them enough to remove the school from the turnaround list. In our planning, we had to reconcile addressing real academic performance with increasing the number of points students were earning on the official paper-and-pencil test.

LOOKING BEYOND TEST SCORES: WHAT DEVELOPING THE WHOLE STUDENT REALLY MEANS

Getting the schools to come to grips with the totality of learning required for proficiency proved to be an effective first step in turning around school culture, but it was only a first step. It generated success, scores went up, and teachers and students could talk about what they were learning and doing. PLC discussions could focus on the quality of the student product, but we couldn't yet focus on cause unless the cause was that the student had not learned the content or the content hadn't been taught.

Getting the schools to come to grips with the totality of learning required for proficiency proved to be an effective first step in turning around school culture, but it was only a first step.

Moving to the next step, where teachers could intentionally build proficiency, required more research on our part and further changes in school cultures and school practice. Eventually, we found a solution by defining assessment proficiency not in terms of test scores but rather in terms of the characteristics that proficient performers take into testing situations. We identified five areas or characteristics related to proficient performance or, at least, to performance at the level of student potential. We still use this five-legged model in our work. In essence, the model is characterized by these five competencies:

1. The proficient student will have to learn (not just be exposed to) the content, task, and level of work expected to get full credit for a performance or answer (*knowledge base*).

2. The proficient student will have to be willing to make an effort to learn and to take the task or test seriously and invest a "best effort" in every question (*attitude base*).

3. The proficient student will have to know what proficient work looks like and how to produce it, and the student must have confidence in his or her ability to work at the level required (*perception base*).

4. The proficient student will have to do the thinking required to understand a task and then completely and accurately perform within it (*thinking base*).

5. The proficient student will have prior success in working at the level of the task (*experience base*).

The five-legged model made it possible for us to define where we needed to be with each student by the time he or she took the test. We assumed this might be a hard sell because teachers were already struggling with an expanded knowledge base, but in actuality, it was easier to sell than the extended unpacking. Teachers immediately understood what the five legs meant and how they applied to individual students. By the end of the first workshop, most teachers were already identifying students who had attitude and perception problems. In one of the workshops, our presenter was taken aback when teachers chose to skip going out to lunch because they wanted an immediate introduction to what we do with this knowledge.

The five-legged model, for the first time, enabled us to look at student work and begin to establish causes of imperfect performance and more insightfully probe student status to determine "where we are." We could identify what the students needed to know, what they needed to be able to do, the level at which they should be working, and their status with respect to each of the supporting characteristics needed for them to work at optimum levels. By this point, we had a practical description of the competencies or characteristics that supported test proficiency and had redefined what "developing the whole student" meant.

The five-legged model allowed us to look at student work and, if the work was not proficient or was significantly below the student's potential, identify the factors that were causing the student to perform at a particular level. Unfortunately, we found that in cases where students were seriously underperforming, there were multiple causal factors involved. This created problems as we tried to prioritize student support. Further research indicated that when multiple problems existed, there was an intervention priority sequence:

1. We were somewhat surprised that *attitude* was a top priority when the student's attitude got in the way of his or her learning or performing. A negative attitude not only undermined learning

and performing, but it also interfered with efforts to support and improve student performance.

2. Student *perceptions*, especially the students' perceptions of self, which are closely tied to attitude, also have a positive or a negative impact on student performance. As early as first grade, some students develop negative perceptions of self and of learning. These perceptions impact their learning and performing until they are addressed.

3. The student's *knowledge* of concepts and tasks has to be equal to the expectations of an assessment, or the student will not perform proficiently. The knowledge base has to be intentionally developed to include all the learnings expected on an assessment.

4. *Thinking* is close or related to the knowledge base and thinking about content is required for students to create meaning for what they're learning. Critical thinking is required on every test question on the state exam, and most questions require multiple thinking steps. The student has to critically read the question, access long-term memory for the content required and perform the tasks embedded in the question proficiently to demonstrate his or her knowledge.

5. The *experience base* is critical because we can't teach many of the competencies that are required of students. Students develop these competencies as they engage in learning work and performing work. We can teach to them, and we can provide work that requires them and then monitor student performance. We can also provide them with strategies for doing competencies more efficiently, but to own the competency, the students have to engage intellectually in learning or performing work.

Once we got to this point, we found that we could identify priority causal elements and begin a search for intentional solutions. We could identify issue areas for individual students, prioritize the student needs, and address those needs with some precision.

This enabled us to find relevant research for both short-term and long-term strategic planning and identify quick-fix Band-Aids. These strategies allowed us to discuss individual students and the quality of their work in PLCs and to develop a priority list for each student. It also enabled us to work with PLC groups to check the implementation and impact of student-focused plans. For several years, this was enough to enable almost all the schools we worked with to target and prepare individual students for success and to make gains on their test scores.

As school cultures changed to embrace this approach of developing proficient students, teachers began to look for more strategies. Initially, they focused on teacher strategies and on materials, but by influencing them to watch students learn in the classroom and evaluate the work students did as learners and then as performers on a test, we could help them to come to grips with the importance of not just teacher work but also student work.

This research changed several things in our conventional wisdom as a turnaround school support group. We learned that high-level engagement does not mean that students are highly engaged in something they enjoy. This was one of the mistakes that we made when we first worked with this in middle-school program development. What's required now is that students be highly engaged intellectually in two different types of work: learning work and performing work. It's important to understand that the teacher cannot do this work for the student. The student must do it. The teacher's role is to prepare and facilitate the student as a worker. This is important. Students can't learn unless they acquire and organize learning and memory. The teacher can't do that for them. More importantly, the teacher can't teach anything but the knowledge base. The student develops the other four legs of the five-legged model through his or her experiences as learner and performer. This means that we not only have to plan a *taught curriculum* to address the content and task components, but we have to attend to the *experienced curriculum* to address the other four legs.

Much of the knowledge base and all the attitude, perception, thinking, and experience bases can only be developed through student engagement and quality work. The student must learn, and the student has to perform. It is student work that will prepare students for both of those tasks. Again, we thought this might be a tough sell in working with staff members who were already over-worked, but that didn't turn out to be the case. When we facilitated the teachers' planning units by developing cognitive and noncognitive goals and then by building student work and student experience to develop a student mastery of those goals, we found that the teachers became excited about using a totally different way to prepare lessons planned around student work rather than teacher work.

Much of the knowledge base and all the attitude, perception, thinking, and experience bases can only be developed through student engagement and quality work.

Expanding the school culture to embrace the five-legged model and the importance of student work led to several changes in the schools:

- School test performance no longer involved a blame game. We could be proactive and focused on getting our students where they needed to be.

- Anonymous test scores were translated into individual students who had different priority needs and needed different supports, allowing us to be very intentional about how we differentiated classroom work and support systems.

- Students and student work became the focus of content-area classrooms.

- Schools started planning courses, units, and lessons in ways that made "planning backward and delivering forward" meaningful concepts.

- Learning work and performing work were structured to yield diagnostic information about student status.

- PLC discussions focused on samples of imperfect learning work and imperfect performing work and identified specifically where student work broke down, why it broke down, and what had to be done with students who weren't learning or performing proficiently.

- Student monitoring strategies were expanded beyond just giving grades and included student status in each of the five competency areas.

- Teacher monitoring strategies no longer involved merely evaluating what the teacher did but focused on the students in the classroom and how the teacher engaged them in doing the learning and performing work required of them.

The five-legged model is now one of the core pieces of our company's intellectual property. It became very popular in schools where we worked, and when we do end-of-year assessments of our performance as a company, we find that, in most cases, teachers identify the model and the student work component as the top two factors that changed their practice.

PRACTITIONER'S NOTE

The tool kit for chapter 2 includes two activities critical for changing the way in which lessons and lesson plans are approached: an *Unpacking a Standard set* and a *Cheat Sheet for the Five-Legged Model.*

UNPACKING A STANDARD — STEP 1

Subject Area: **Grade Level:**   **Unpacking Team:**

Standards Statement:

Concepts/Relationships	Tasks	Test Question Types

UNPACKING A STANDARD — STEP 2

Subject Area: _____   Grade Level: _____   Unpacking Team: _____

Standards Statement: _____

Concepts/Relationships

Tasks

Critical Learning	Located in Our Materials/ Curricula	Critical Task	Located in Our Materials/ Curricula

PLANNING TO PLAN — UNIT GOALS

Subject: **Unit:**   **Teacher(s):**   **Date:**

At the end of this unit, all students will learn, understand, and demonstrate mastery of the following:

Concepts/Relationships		Tasks		End-of-Unit Testing
New	*Reinforced*	*New*	*Reinforced*	*Types of Questions/ Number*

Subject: _____   Unit: _____   Teacher(s): _____   Date: _____

Unit Duration		Number of Lessons Committed		Formative and Summative Monitoring
Start Date	End Date	Lesson Sequence	Focus	Monitoring Progress Plan
				Formative/Date	Summative/Date

THE FIVE-LEGGED MODEL OF EDUCATION

Knowledge: State assessments establish expectations for all students. Each student must own the learnings (concepts, tasks, thinking) required to meet these expectations. This critical vocabulary needs to be operational, not just known.

Attitude: Students must know the learning required, but that is not enough; they must be *willing* to perform the tasks required and invest a "best effort" on every part of the assessment. Every answer or product should represent the student's *personal best effort*.

Perception: Most state assessments embed perceptions generated by learning. There are two perceptions required for student performance that are not related to standard expectations:

1. **Perception of Proficiency:** The student knows what constitutes good work and how to produce it.

2. **Perception of Efficacy:** The student believes, "I can work successfully at the levels required."

Thinking: Mature thinking patterns and critical reading and writing are required on every question of a state test.

Experience: Almost all students need two sets of experiences; they must have work experience that forms the five legs, and they must have experience working successfully at the level of the assessment. In other words, they must have both formative and calibrating experiences.

	Why It Is Important	*Problem Causes*
Leg 1: Knowledge	State assessments establish expectations for all students. To meet these expectations, each student must own the learnings (concepts, tasks, thinking) required. This vocabulary must not only be known but must be operational.	If the critical learnings are not known or are not operational, students cannot perform required tasks. This knowledge base must be congruent to the task for the students to reach their potential. Alternative languages and level experiences can produce a gap between potential and performance.
Leg 2: Attitude	The students must know the learnings required, but that is not enough. They must be willing to perform the tasks required and invest their best effort on every part of the assessment. The expectation is that every answer or product represents the students' personal best effort.	Poor attitude usually causes a student to learn and perform below potential. It leads to a number of problems: • Low motivation • Attention problems • Inefficient use of time • Loss of concentration • Sabotage
Leg 3: Perceptions	Most state assessments embed perceptions (time, space, distance and so on). Two perceptions that are required but are not related to standard expectations are: • Perception of proficiency: Knowing what constitutes good work and how to produce it. • Perception of efficacy: The belief that "I can work successfully at the level required." Students must know what good work is and believe that they can produce it, or they will not demonstrate to their potential.	Students operate in a comfort zone built by experience as a learner. If a student believes that poor work or inadequate effort is good enough, she or he will work at that level on any assessment. If the student believes that she or he cannot do the work required, she or he will be correct. Lack of belief in self produces anxiety and can negatively impact attitude.
Leg 4: Thinking	Mature thinking patterns and critical reading/writing/thinking are required on every question of a state test.	Immature thinkers, impulsive responders, and attention deficit students regularly misread questions, leave tasks unfinished, and produce products that lack depth and integrity.
Leg 5: Experience	Almost all students need two sets of experiences. They must have work experience that forms the five supporting legs, and they must have experience working successfully at the level of the assessment. They must have formative and calibrating experiences, where differentiation and accommodation become critical.	If the student lacks the appropriate experience, she or he can know the content but be unprepared to work at the required levels.

Notes:

_____

_____

_____

_____

_____

_____

_____

_____

_____

_____

_____

_____

_____

_____

_____

_____

_____

_____

_____

_____

_____

_____

03

BEYOND THE TEST: DEALING WITH SUCCESSFUL TRANSITION

In 2008, some of the ED staff had the opportunity to listen to several critics of public education describe their problems with the products of the K–12 system. The consensus was that public education produced students underprepared for a successful transition to life beyond school. This was problematic for us because it added a serious new element to the idea of proficiency. They weren't talking about proficiency on a test. They were talking about readiness to apply learning in real-world or advanced academic situations. It was also problematic because when we probed to find out what it was the students were lacking, we couldn't get a definitive answer. When we took our notes from the conference to schools, we were surprised that the schools agreed. The high schools were sure that students came to high school unprepared, while the middle schools said the elementary schools were doing an inadequate job of building student preparation for middle school and the elementary schools said that parents were not doing their part to get the students ready for kindergarten. When we probed, we again found that teachers could not give us a definitive answer to the question of what their students were lacking. When we tried to pin these answers down, using the five-legged model to determine the where students were seriously lacking, we were able to get a better picture of what we were dealing with, but many responses still included, "But it's more than that."

When state legislatures started taking this seriously and legislated "successful transitions," we had to think beyond the five-legged model. In two states, we had the opportunity to talk to critics from different walks of life about what they expected from students coming into their particular area of interest. In talking with these teachers, business leaders, college professors, trade school instructors, and military recruiters about what readiness meant and why they thought many students were not ready, it became obvious that, while each group had different expectations, none required only test prepared-ness. For some, social competencies were most important; for others, thinking and mental habits were more important. All groups talked about learning and working traits and what is now identified as social and emotional intelligences. *No one talked about specific content knowledge.*

In talking with these teachers, business leaders, college professors, trade school instructors, and military recruiters about what readiness meant and why they thought many students were not ready, it became obvious that, while each group had different expectations, none required only test preparedness.

Creating successful transitions required us to talk not just about successful scores on a paper-and-pencil assessment but also about those proficiencies enabling a student to transition successfully from one grade to another in school and from K–12 education to the postsecondary world. Currently, we are researching nine proficiency areas that we believe relate to successful transitions to postsecondary education or to the workforce:

Assessment Proficiency is required since tests are still used to judge student proficiency. Students still have to know, and successfully work with, what they understand at the level of the assessment as described in our five-legged model. As long as schools are responsible for tracking student growth and measuring student proficiency with paper-and-pencil tests, this proficiency set will be required of all students.

Academic Competency (skills, habits of mind, and behaviors that enable the student to be successful in school and other academic settings) was overlooked at first because we focused on assessment performance. Conventional wisdom assumes students already know how to learn — if only they would study. We found a set of academic proficiencies were required for a successful transition from one academic level to the next. The list includes setting and pursuing goals, demonstrating learning orally and in writing, framing and answering questions, organizing time and meeting deadlines, following directions and completing tasks, and meeting teacher, school, and district expectations.

Learning Competence (skills, habits of mind and attitudes that enable a student to be an independent learner in academic and real-world settings) is required for academic and test-taking success and is demanded in transitions from secondary school to college, work, or the military. Learning proficiency is evidenced by a student's active listening, critical reading, critical thinking, critical writing, effective note-taking, task analysis, focus on the exercise at hand, acquisition of new learning, organization of new learning into memory, creation of meaning for new learning, self-monitoring of learning and performance, and independent initiation and pursuit of learning without specific direction.

Thinking Proficiency (habits of mind and thinking processes related to critical thinking, creative thinking, and knowledge application) is expected in academic progression and required in transition to postsecondary life. Different thinking gurus approach this proficiency from different directions. We are currently looking at habits of mind that support other proficiencies and at specific thinking strategies and skills identified by the thinking gurus. Thinking proficiencies include critical reading, critical writing, and critical reasoning; formulating, defending, and attacking arguments; convergent and divergent thinking; using and testing logic; being thoughtful in approaching tasks; and collecting, organizing, analyzing, and communicating data.

Communication Proficiency (the ability to communicate effectively in both oral and written venues) was a primary concern of all postsecondary groups, though K–12 teachers emphasized writing in particular. Our research in this area indicated that communication proficiency must include — at least — active listening, effective speaking, critical reading and writing, and integrating visual elements and technology into a student's communication.

Work Proficiency (the ability to understand, plan for, and successfully complete tasks and the attitudes and perceptions that support these abilities) was required by all groups. The ability to engage in a task at high levels, maintain high-level engagement, and follow tasks to completion was identified as a serious transition issue by all groups, K–12 and beyond. This proficiency includes paying attention to details, monitoring progress and adapting as needed, listening to or reading directions, and following those directions accurately.

Social Proficiency (the ability to learn and work effectively, interact effectively with others, and build effective relationships with coworkers and the attitudes and perceptions that support successful social interactions) was the most-mentioned area by postsecondary groups. All the groups we interviewed found students had trouble working in learning-and-working team situations. There seemed to be little understanding of the etiquette, mores, and taboos associated with peer work teams. In jobs, the military, and upper-level university situations, the ability to work as an effective team member is fundamental to successful learning and task completion.

Emotional proficiency is the least understood of the proficiencies listed here and yet the one most identified as a problem area for students having difficulty in making transitions from one grade level to the next.

Emotional Proficiency (the ability to control emotional responses and to act/react in ways that enhance individual and group performance) was the area considered most problematic for students who failed to make a successful transition to the next grade in a K–12 setting. It also appeared to be an issue in the first two years of college and in the military. Emotional maturity includes the ability to interact with adults and peers in a way that will enhance learning or task completion. Emotional proficiency is the least understood of the proficiencies listed here and yet the one most identified as a problem area for students having difficulty in making transitions from one grade level to the next.

World Awareness (knowledge of sufficient current events, science, economics, geography, politics, and history to make informed decisions in real-world situations) was a priority for some postsecondary teachers, all military recruiters, and most business responders. The postsecondary groups talked about the need for a well-rounded worker or student and how they needed their students and workers to ground the learning or the task in real-world terms. As one military recruiter pointed out, "You can't make it in the world if you don't know what's going on around you."

Dealing with any of these competencies requires a change of focus. It requires us to rethink and redefine what our curriculum must provide and produce. Of course, schools will still need to prepare students for high-stakes tests because that will continue to be a measure of accountability. But in addition, they will have to look at the proficiencies beyond content knowledge and assessment and delve into areas of social, cognitive, and emotional proficiency. They will have to rethink performance gaps in terms other than just test scores. Action research keyed to students' priority needs will have to be included in every school plan, and data beyond the whole group's test scores will need to be collected and analyzed. Improvement at this level requires changes in the culture, climate, learning environment, and work (for both teachers and students).

The investigation into what's expected of students caused us to change several our preconceptions about standards-based education:

- We do not teach standards; rather, we teach to standard expectations. The focus is not on covering the content, but on building a student who can be proficient on assessments and prepared to make successful transitions.

- Standards and expectations must be unpacked completely. Departmental and grade-level discussions must focus on what the whole learner needs to look like by the end of the academic year. Standards require a common understanding of what proficiency means and a means of tracking that proficiency across content areas and from grade level to grade level.

- We must look beyond the standard statements for the learning sets we have to address. Test specifications, sample tests, and materials have to be unpacked as well. In addition, school leaders will have to assess the whole competency set expected for students to be successful test takers and make successful transitions.

- The noncurricular competencies cannot be taught *per se*; they are developed from student experiences as a learner and performer and are a part of an experienced curriculum rather than a taught curriculum.

- Critical reading, writing, and thinking must be embedded in all pre-K–12 classrooms.

- Teachers must understand the importance of student experience — in relation not just to the learning and performing proficiencies but also to all the proficiencies that are expected for successful transitions as well.

- School leaders have to rethink issues of equity, ability, and disability. Once we understand the importance of student experience, we have to accept that providing students with equal experiences creates unequal performance and unequal transition. For example, allowing only natural leaders or vocal students to do all the leading in a class excludes the majority of students from the competency-building impact of being a leader.

If classrooms are organized solely around the delivery of content, and not the broader set of competencies enabling proficient learning and performing, schools will remain at the mercy of factors other than content knowledge in determining which students will be successful on assessments and which will make successful transitions.

Currently, ED is studying education reform in three states to determine how the school-to-work initiative is going to impact education practice. We are concerned that there seems to be the expectation that if we get the students to do certain activities, they will develop the "soft skills" needed to make a successful transition into the job market. In our mind, there's a difference between doing the activity that is provided in a curriculum and doing an intentional work sequence that's designed to encourage the development of habits of mind, specific thinking or working competencies, or specific social interaction patterns. For us, it's important that schools identify the package of competencies that are supposed to deliver and intentionally develop experiences for students in and outside the classroom that will produce those competencies.

Practitioner's Note

Included in the tool kit are tools that ED coaches use to focus PLC discussions on student competencies. The tools for chapter 3 include a worksheet for developing a profile of competencies on each student and a worksheet for determining the point at which work breaks down.

Student Competency Profile

Date: **Student:**   **Teacher:**

Proficiency	Academic Proficiency	Social Proficiency	Emotional Proficiency	Thinking Proficiency	Assessment Proficiency	Learning Proficiency	Working Proficiency	Thinking Proficiency	Communication Proficiency	World Awareness
Confirmed										
Next Steps										

Analysis of Student Work for Point of Breakdown

Student: **Work Sample:**   **Learning Impact Tool:**

Student	Multiple Choice	Short Answer	Extended Response	Word Problem	On-Demand Writing	Real-World Application	Response to Data
The student was prepared and started in a timely fashion.							
The student critically read or listened and understood with precision what had to be done.							
The student was highly engaged in the work or task from beginning to completion.							
The student completed all the required activities.							
The student regularly checked his or her work to make sure he or she was on the right track.							
The quality of the student work was adequate for the student product to be considered acceptable.							
The learning impact of the task was assessed, and the student learning was adequate.							

Action Plan for Student

Top Priority	Adult Responsible	Action Steps	Learning Impact Tool/Date

Notes:

_____

_____

_____

_____

_____

_____

_____

_____

_____

_____

_____

_____

_____

_____

_____

_____

_____

_____

_____

_____

_____

_____

_____

_____

04

WHY AREN'T WE REACHING OUR GOALS? DETERMINING ROOT CAUSE

The work we did in defining test proficiency and competencies needed for successful transitions caused us to rethink other parts of our conventional wisdom. When our work began, we assumed that if students missed a question, it indicated they did not know the content. If they didn't make successful transitions, it was because they weren't prepared academically to make successful transitions. Now, we realize this was at best a grossly inadequate assumption.

AHA MOMENT — CONTENT

As we worked through the sample test report mentioned in chapter 1, we encountered another *aha*. We found students for whom content wasn't the major issue. We found issues with curriculum. Some of the content had not been taught before the test, and some students had never seen some of the types of questions that they had to answer on the test. In other cases, we were unable to identify why the student missed the question. As long as we relied strictly on test scores and on discussions with teachers about the test scores, even if we did an effective red-flag analysis, we found the following:

- We couldn't relate any of our discussions to where the students' work broke down.

- We couldn't identify the cause of the breakdown.

- Without this information, all our planning was guesswork.

- Without this information, our data collection was random and couldn't be related to the real issues that caused students to perform poorly on a test.

- Academic planning, especially the planning of student work, could only focus on the content — vocabulary and task — required of students.

- Support programs remained accidental, and students were grouped by label or score rather than by priority need.

Some of the content had not been taught before the test, and some students had never seen some of the types of questions that they had to answer on the test.

As a follow-up to our initial evaluation of the state test report, we gave a brief test to the current students. Then, we analyzed student responses on the test and compared their responses to the work they did as learners immediately before the test. We found, in many cases, students missed questions because the work they had done as learners was not adequate to prepare them for the question. Other students who answered incorrectly or performed poorly read the question incorrectly and either answered the wrong question correctly or simply missed the question. Still others ran out of time and guessed on the last few questions. This level of probing identified *what* the students did wrong but did not answer the *why*.

AHA MOMENT — DETERMINING CAUSE

This led us to our second *aha* moment. To determine cause, we had to observe the student working and maybe even talk to the student about why he or she made certain choices or answered in a specific way. We couldn't rely on the scores to give us this information nor could we derive this information from patterns we identified in our red-flag analysis. To determine cause, we had to deal with individual students as they performed or with their teachers who observed them performing and knew enough about the students to begin the process of determining the cause and point of breakdown. To plan intentionally to build student learners and student performers, we needed to know where nonproficient work broke down and why it broke down at that point.

To determine cause, we had to observe the student working and maybe even talk to the student about why he or she made certain choices or answered in a specific way.

As we probed using the five-legged model and talked to teachers and students, we found that we were dealing with several issues that caused students who knew the content to perform poorly. Because we were hired to improve student scores, we always focused first on test performance. Because teachers assumed the students did not know the content if they missed the question, we started by assessing the knowledge base of the students. Of the five legs in the model, the knowledge base is the easiest performance issue to use to get teachers' attention. If we ruled that leg out, we forced them to consider that other issues (or legs) could be the problem.

As we probed using the five-legged model and talked to teachers and students, we found that we were dealing with several issues that caused students who knew the content to perform poorly.

PERFORMANCE ISSUES: THE KNOWLEDGE BASE

Three elements make up the knowledge base of state tests. Conceptual vocabulary is the language of the standard. It includes concepts and relationships (the nouns), tasks (the verbs), and the level of engagement required. In addition, the knowledge base includes processes that are critical to student performance on a test. These include critical reading (recreational reading strategies are inadequate), critical and creative thinking, and critical writing or speaking. If any of these knowledgebase elements are missing or undeveloped, the student can own the other elements and still miss questions. We found students who did the following:

- Missed questions because they learned a language parallel that was not congruent to the language tested. They didn't know they knew the answer.

- Knew the content but could not perform the task.

- Could perform the task but not at the level required on the test.

- Misread questions and answered the wrong question.

- Could not follow all the thinking steps required in a question.

- Read too slowly to finish the test.

- Did not have a strategy for doing a critical read.

- Could not write in a way demonstrating their thinking about a prompt.

The knowledge base is necessary for student success on a test. Students must know the content, the relationships, the tasks, and the level of performance required if they are going to demonstrate what they can do on a test. Unfortunately, the knowledge base is not sufficient to guarantee student performance to the level of their potential.

PERFORMANCE ISSUES: THE ATTITUDE BASE

When we looked for cause, we did not identify attitude as an issue until late in our discussions. It was only after attitude showed up time after time in teacher and student discussions as the cause of performance that we came to understand it may be the most important of the five legs in shaping students as learners and performers after the third grade.

In the beginning, we assumed that every student gave us his or her best effort on a test, especially on a state test. To make the assumptions we did about who needed support and what support they needed, this had to be the case. Unfortunately, it wasn't. We found students' attitudes determined what work they would do and wouldn't do in class as learners. We found attitude determined how engaged the students would get in classwork or in test work, the level of thinking they would apply to a task, how they would work with peers or teachers in learning activities, and how much effort they would invest in learning work and tests.

In addition, we found attitude affects attendance, behavior in class, relationships with teachers and peers, the attention span of students during class or tests, and the willingness of students to self-assess and seek support when needed. We found that, around third grade, attitude became critical to student success. Without addressing bad or negative attitudes, we could make little headway in developing the other legs of the five. Still, while attitude is necessary and critical, it is not, in itself, sufficient to guarantee proficient performance. The perception base relates to attitude, and in some research, is linked to a cause-and-effect relationship important to student success.

PERFORMANCE ISSUES: THE PERCEPTION BASE

There are several perceptions that come into play in a learning or testing situation. Two of them are critical in our discussion:

- *The perception of proficiency* is the student's understanding of what proficiency requires, what it looks like, how much work it takes, and what that work requires. It must be owned by students before they can seek to be proficient.

- *The perception of self as a professional performer,* the students' understanding of proficiency and ability to do the work and demonstrate the knowledge, is required for them to develop the confidence and work ethic needed to be independent and proficient learners and performers.

We found in our work with schools that students who struggle with learning and performing were frequently given support systems that involve off-level learning work, off-level assessments, and off-level materials. Frequently, students used language and strategies appropriate for lower grade levels than that appropriate for their current grade level. They had assessments that included less-challenging test items, and they received *alternative* ways to earn good grades. In these situations, it was easy for students to develop a perception of proficiency inconsistent with the proficiencies required on a grade-level-appropriate test. Even if they gave the test their best effort, the perception of proficiency they developed with their off-level work caused them to work below the level required on a level-appropriate assessment. In this case, their low performance was caused partially by adult decisions about what the students should do in class. *Their class prepared them to perform below their potential.*

The student's perception of himself or herself as a learner can be developed in a variety of ways. By the end of first grade, many students realize they're given work that isn't as challenging as the work other students are doing, and by third grade, the students understand they can't do the work other students are doing. They develop a perception of self that embraces off-level performance.

Other students with physical or mental challenges may assume they can't work at the same level as other students. Students with attention problems know they can't work as long or hard as other students and they won't get the amount of attention that hardworking students do. So, as a consequence, they frequently begin to act out to get the attention they want. Students who struggle in a particular content area (particularly reading and math) early in school assume that that struggle will continue and they will never be good in that particular content area. This will be true even if they change as they mature and develop the capability to master the content area. Their perception of self will become a reality because the student will live out that perception. Students who assume they will be poor test-takers will be poor test takers unless we change that perception.

Through research, we also find that perception of "self" works in the opposite direction of improving performance. Some students come to believe they are good readers and good students because their teachers nurture their performance. In this case, several things can happen. Students can believe they are good readers and then, in the middle of a test, find out they have no idea what they are reading or how to go about reading text for the purpose required. Some students only understand recreational reading and have no concept of critical or close reading, which is what is required on all state assessments.

Another problem related to the perception of self is teacher dependence. Many students come to understand they can do their best work when the teacher nurtures them, gives assistance, or begins the thinking process for them. These students develop a working comfort zone that includes the teacher as initiator. When the teacher cannot initiate or is not present, they will not or cannot operate to their potential as performers. Immature students or those who have difficulties and require teacher assistance to overcome, frequently become teacher-dependent responders and will not reach their potential without the teacher's presence.

PERFORMANCE ISSUES: THE THINKING BASE

The thinking base is one we knew would be problematic, yet we still underestimated its importance. Every test requires multiple thinking steps in every question — even multiple choice. Every test question requires a thoughtful/critical reading of the question and any text or visual prompt included. An impulsive reader or impulsive responder will miss questions even when he or she knows the content.

When we looked into the research on thinking, we found successful/proficient students have thoughtful habits of mind (e.g., seeking clarity), a variety of critical-thinking strategies, a perception of strategies for creative thinking, divergent and convergent thinking, and thoughtful reading, writing, listening, and speaking. Most of these are required on state tests today.

If we don't embed a thinking strand in our curriculum, we can produce students who know and remember content but can't use the content in a thoughtful response to a prompt.

Developing thoughtful students requires that we teach about thinking, teach for thinking, and teach with thinking. If we don't embed a thinking strand in our curriculum, we can produce students who know and remember content but can't use the content in a thoughtful response to a prompt. Today, we encourage schools to do the following:

- Unpack the thinking requirements of each grade level and embed those thinking requirements in the curriculum

- Build a thinking strand in all content areas and monitor the students' progress as thinkers

- Prepare teachers to be leaders of thinkers as well as deliverers of content

- Analyze the thinking required on state and district tests and prepare the students to think in those ways and at those levels

- Include thinking-focused questions on all teacher-made tests and monitor for points of breakdown and causes of breakdown

Many students can learn the content to perform tasks and can remember them for teacher-made tests, but these same students cannot step out of the comfort zone of the teacher-made unit test into a cumulative test of the whole year's content. Such students lack fundamental habits of mind and thinking strategies that enable them to operate independently from long-term memory without teacher cues being present. The students will fail to perform to their potential on state end-of-year tests.

PERFORMANCE ISSUES: THE EXPERIENCE BASE

When we think about curriculum in a school or classroom, we usually think in terms of the taught curriculum. When we look at what's expected of students, however, we understand that, while the taught curriculum is necessary, it is not sufficient to meet the needs of all students or all student learning styles. In terms of the five legs, the taught curriculum develops the knowledge base and a small part of the thinking base. The other legs are developed in a different way.

There is another curriculum called the experienced curriculum, which is developed as the students interact with learning and performing work in the classroom. Attitude, perception, and thinking are to a great extent developed only through the experiences the student goes through as a learner and performer. When the student becomes a product of the experienced curriculum, this creates several problems for us as turnaround agents:

- Most teachers don't know about or understand the five-legged model or the experienced curriculum.

- Without this understanding, teachers allow students to participate unequally in the experiences offered in the classroom. This creates experience inequity, causing performance gaps when the students have approximately the same level of understanding of the content. Question-and-answer patterns are usually referred to as examples of how some students are able to participate and others do not.

- Without an understanding of what's expected of students, teachers develop accidental experiences. Only those students who highly engage in the experiences actually benefit from them. Other students do not.

- Students operate in a *comfort zone* that's formed by their experiences as workers in a classroom. If their comfort zone is not consistent with the assessment that they're given, they will be unable to reach their potential. Comfort zones are established by the experienced curriculum.

- In research, writers refer to the "rule of equivalent experience" that reads that learners must work at the level of the test, understand that this is the level of the test, and receive feedback that tells them where they stand in terms of the test expectations.

NONCOGNITIVE ISSUES

In addition to the five-legged model and the cognitive issues connected with it, there are several cognitive and noncognitive issues that we identified as possible causes of poor performance:

- The speed of thoughtful or purposeful reading can be a major impediment. If there's a significant gap between the students' recreational reading rate and their critical reading rate, it can cause them to fail to complete the test because they simply can't read fast enough to answer all the questions. Many students who can read score poorly on reading tests because they have little experience with critical reading and have not developed an adequate critical reading rate.

- Maturity level plays a part in determining an intervention. Immature students may not be able to perform grade-appropriate thinking or presenting tasks.

- Attendance is an issue. If students miss five days of class, it will affect their performance. Missing 10 days will have a significant impact on performance on a test, while missing 20 days or more can cause a student to perform at less than 50 percent of his or her potential.

- Attention span and classroom disruptions are also considerations. State tests regularly require students as young as the third grade to stay engaged in questions for 3-15 minutes, or in the case of writing, for 45 minutes. For many students, especially those who are immature, this level of engagement is not possible. Their attention span will not support it.

- Classroom disruptions (tardiness, misbehavior, disturbances outside the class, and so on) compound this problem, especially when they occur during the test. A disruption not only destroys the attention span for the duration of the disruption; it also breaks the rhythm of the lesson of the test. It will take many students time after the disruption is over to get back on task and reestablish their thinking.

- Gender differences should be considered when talking about achieving maximum performance from students — boys need more personal space; girls respond to personal attention, and so on. Failure to understand and accommodate gender differences can cause students to operate below their potential.

WHAT THIS MEANS FOR EDUCATORS

We struggled then and continued to struggle with teachers who insist on doing activities the kids really like or activities they "saw in a workshop" that "sounded good." For us to help students improve as performers and thus increase their test scores, we have to help them build a sound performance base. They must have the attitudes, perceptions, knowledge, thinking patterns, and experience base necessary to reach their potential. Without those, we can't sustain student gains over time and will have to continue to rely on yearly Band-Aids. In addition, we have to identify cognitive and noncognitive conditions that can cause students to underperform if we truly want to move all students from where they are to where they are expected to be by year-end.

We are at a point in our company where we believe that if we have access to a school staff early in the year and can get them involved in unpacking the standards to establish expectations, help them develop a perception of the five-legged model and plan to identify issues within the five legs as well as provide experiences that will remediate those issues, we can improve the scores in any school. It will require hard work, and it will require that the teachers and the administrators come to grips with their preconceived assumptions and abandon them when necessary as we had to do.

What we do know is if we do not attempt to develop the five legs that support learning and performing and the competencies that relate to successful transitions, we are making *adult-focused decisions* that will put students at risk; these things are part of the expectation package spelled out in all state standards and assessments. If we fail to identify and address noncognitive issues that impact students, we are allowing student performance to be reduced by conditions that we can control.

PRACTITIONER'S NOTE

The tool kit at the end of chapter 4 is intended to encourage educators to look for cause as well as the point of breakdown. It includes a cognitive and noncognitive checklist, a student independence log, a school readiness checklist, a "student as learner" checklist, and a "student as performer" checklist.

COGNITIVE AND NONCOGNITIVE CHECKLIST

Concerns

Characteristic	Yes	Notes
Attitude Problem		
Attention Problem		
Work Ethic Problem		
Informal Language		
Endurance Problem		
Little Home Support		
Impulsive Behavior		
Behavior Problem		
Low Expectations		
Little Language Experience		
Low Self-Esteem		
Negative Peer Group		

Concerns

Characteristic	Yes	Notes
Attendance Problem		
Easily Led Astray		
Demanding Attention		
Physical/Mental Issue		

Positives

Characteristic	Yes	Notes
Independent		
Attentive		
Long-Term Memory		
Critical Vocabulary		
Format Master		
Critical Reading		
Critical Thinking		

Positives

Characteristic	Yes	Notes
Critical Writing		
Operating Vocabulary		
Experience		
Good Attitude		
Good Work Ethic		
Perception		
Work Revision		
Supportive Home		
High Expectations		
Positive Peer Group		

Special Notes:

_____

_____

_____

_____

_____

_____

What Worked:

_____

_____

_____

_____

_____

_____

STUDENT INDEPENDENCE LOG

Student	Truly Independent	Independent in Comfort Zone	Independent after Teacher Initiation	Limited Ongoing Support Needed	Extensive Ongoing Support Needed

STUDENT READINESS

Student	Attends school regularly with fewer than five absences or tardies	Exhibits level-appropriate behavior and thinking patterns	Controls attention and stays on task during learning work or assessments	Is an active listener and critical reader	Reading rate, fluency, and comprehension levels are appropriate for the grade level	Communicates thinking effectively in oral and written exercises

STUDENT AS LEARNER

Student	Succeeded in learning in previous years	Learns and works independently	Acquires, organizes, and creates meaning for class learnings	Follows directions and completes tasks	Links learning to prior learning	Acquires and uses discipline-specific language

STUDENT AS PERFORMER

Student	Succeeded in performing in previous years	Approaches assessment in a thoughtful/ thinking manner	Is self-critical, revises work, and seeks assistance when needed	Gives best effort on all assessments and maintains effort through the assessment	Performs proficiently orally, in writing, and through technology	Accepts shaping feedback and uses feedback to improve performance

Notes:

_____

_____

_____

_____

_____

_____

_____

_____

_____

_____

_____

_____

_____

_____

_____

_____

_____

_____

_____

_____

05

PROGRESS MONITORING: MEASURING WHOSE PROGRESS TOWARD WHAT?

Establishing what was expected of students as *proficient performers* not only helped us plan student and teacher work but also gave direction to our efforts to monitor student (and school) progress. As high-stakes accountability and its dependence on test measures became the norm, efforts to monitor and quantify progress toward goals and objectives increased. Now, no matter where we worked, there were attempts by the state, districts, and schools to monitor progress toward the schools' test-performance targets. Educators took lessons from the industrial and corporate world into the schoolhouse as they attempted to benchmark student performance and track progress toward the goals established in the school turnaround or transformation plan.

Our early experiences with this kind of work proved quite fruitful; the very act of putting achievement numbers on the table makes a school more intentional. We saw charting progress could generate a healthy competitiveness in both students and adults. In the best of cases, it focused and increased effort. We encouraged periodic "scrimmage testing," or summative assessments, to measure the current level of student mastery of standards. We also developed weekly or biweekly, formative assessments to inform classroom instruction.

- However, problems arose as monitoring systems took on greater scope and importance. Creating and managing the systems required for progress monitoring was a tremendous challenge for schools and districts as it required time and resources. Making people accountable for those systems increased the pressure and stress on everyone involved. As a result, we began to see the following:

- Students were taking state-aligned benchmark tests three or more times a year in addition to other quizzes, unit tests, semester tests, and other assessments given by teachers, schools, and districts. If institutions were sophisticated enough, they might triangulate the data to see if the results on one test matched the results on another to learn quite a bit. But this was rare. Too much testing made testing itself the enemy; student effort waned, and teacher attitudes soured. Everyone became test-fatigued.

- Many of the school and district tests used to monitor proficiency had different formats, levels of complexity, or critical vocabularies than the state test, but schools compared results as though it were an apples-to-apples situation. False reads on progress became the norm. In many cases, educators' efforts actually prepared the students to perform below their level of potential.

- The progress tracking involved comparing aggregate school scores. Each test was examined to see if the number of proficient students went up, stayed the same, or went down. Few schools checked individual scores to make sure the students who were proficient on the first test were also proficient on the second test.

- Most systems proved students who did poorly on one test also did poorly on other tests; students who did poorly at one time of the year did poorly at other times as well. However, we could not establish whether students were making progress, staying on the same level, or losing ground.

- Few of the performance-monitoring systems identified what progress meant other than referring to scores decreasing, staying the same, or increasing.

- Few monitoring systems were set up properly as implementation-and-impact studies, which, ideally, would evaluate how a strategy or program was executed and determine if the implementation had the desired impact on teacher or student performance. There was no way of knowing if changes had an impact on the targeted results.

- Under pressure of time and expectations, teachers and administrators sometimes falsified data sets or "fudged" them.

In many cases, educators' efforts actually prepared the students to perform below their level of potential.

What began in most places as a good-faith effort to "know where we stand" evolved into "something we had to do."

Our conventional approach to data management started to change when several of us attended a data management workshop about linking data from different sources. The presenter emphasized that effective management required the ability to link streams and was critical for monitoring the plan-implementation progress from initiation to completion. He described a process including first establishing, with precision, what we wanted and the questions our data needed to answer and then identifying and linking the data streams to tell us what we wanted to know.

After the workshop, we found we didn't agree on what to look for as evidence of progress. In most of our schools, principals checked to see if teachers were implementing what they were told to, and at some point, they checked to see if student scores were going up. However, this information didn't fit the model developed at the workshop.

Another change in our data wisdom occurred when we started comparing notes on what we thought was important from the data workshop and found, in addition to the presenter's emphasis on defining what we wanted to monitor, he also emphasized the need to monitor in a timely fashion. Many times, we rely on data sets so outdated that they cannot be used to inform planning or for decision making. Reluctantly, we regularly used state and district test reports at least months old and sometimes a year old. It took us several discussions to relate tight iteration loops to our monitoring systems.

The presenter's insistence that we collect the data that were actually relevant to what we needed to know necessitated another change. At this time, most of our principals were monitoring the teachers to see if they were implementing the plan, using the right materials, and giving the district tests on time. According to the presenter, they were monitoring the wrong data. If we needed to know about student performance, we needed to be monitoring the students in real time and assessing how the plans being implemented were affecting student work and student product.

Subsequent discussions led us to rethink progress monitoring and develop a more intentional and clearly defined process. In the proficiencies chapter, we mentioned a folk saying about knowing where you are and where you are going before you make a plan. The saying continues: "Once you start your journey, you should check, periodically, to see if you are going where you think you are going." Applying what we learned in the data workshop, we focused on the goals generated for each grade level in the unpacking activity and then used the five-legged model and the competency list to identify the data streams we wanted to follow on every student. This proved to be more complex than the data management systems found in most school plans and was difficult to sell to district IT professionals.

Obviously, we wanted to monitor individual student test performance — this was what we, as a company, were responsible for changing. Philosophically, we felt we needed to measure progress to see if students were learning and performing more effectively in the classrooms. When we started talking about competencies other than test performance competencies, we realized we needed a monitoring menu from which we could pick to individualize the collection of data needed for one specific school. In the end, we built a progress-monitoring tool kit that could track changes in student performance as a learner and test taker.

ESTABLISHING PRIORITY NEEDS

Establishing priority needs didn't happen all at once but developed over time. We started with an evaluation of student learning work or testing work and developed tools that established whether the student performance was proficient. If it were, we tried to identify what worked so we could do it again. If it were not, we identified where the student work broke down and what the student's support priorities needed to be. This allowed us to develop very intentional intervention and support strategies for individual students where we could monitor both the implementation of the strategy and the student's response to the intervention. That in turn gave us the data we needed to check every student's learning and performing work to see if he or she was implementing the support strategies and if those support strategies were indeed improving his or her performance.

Because of the importance of test scores, student test performance was always the core minimum performance we monitored. In many low-performing schools where the capacity of the staff was limited, this might be the only student performance we monitored and supported in the first year. In cases like this, we linked student performance to the learning and assessment work done by the student. We then checked the work to see if it improved. If it did not improve, we probed it to determine where the work broke down and establish why it had at that point. This gave us a firm starting point for our next set of interventions with individual students.

Improving student performance doesn't happen accidentally. We emphasize the following:

- Improving student work requires developing and monitoring the student's work as a learner and performer and not the teacher's work as a lecturer or textbook director.

- Scores must be individualized and personalized. We can't improve 40 percent or 16 novices unless we know the real students represented by those numbers. It is especially important when dealing with state assessment reports that we quantify the aggregate scores, identify the students who scored at each performance level, detect red-flag patterns that can inform discussions, and update by assessing the current performance levels of the students in school during the year.

- Monitoring student assessment work requires more than the use of raw scores. It necessitates a close analysis of the student product to determine if the product is proficient, and if it's not proficient, it requires us to establish the point at which the work broke down.

- Because we are required to build a student into both a learner and a performer, the student work that's monitored needs to include samples of his or her work as a learner and a test-taker (or performer).

- Support for students needs to address the cause of breakdown, not the score or the content area of the work.

- Monitoring needs to be ongoing, and current data need to replace outdated data at a minimum monthly, but ideally, weekly.

- Current data need to drive PLC discussions related to planning student work in units and lessons and support programs designed to meet student needs.

- In a best-case scenario, schools should monitor student growth in both the assessment characteristics (the five-legged model) and the successful transition competencies.

In most schools, we created data rooms where student learning work, monitoring samples, and test work could be collected. In such a situation, PLC groups could link learning work samples to test performance to determine whether student learning and performing improved in that particular learning cycle. Here, teams of teachers could monitor student learning and link it to student performance and then design targeted support and remediation programs.

DATA ROOM CASE STUDY

While working in Florida, we had a unique opportunity to collaborate with the state Department of Education. In many states, outside consultants or state coaches have a negative reputation; they're seen as people with agendas or who make too much of an oversight role. In Florida, we worked with several state and regional executive directors who wanted to experiment with a new model. They tasked us, as external providers, to collaborate with their state coaches in providing schools with the help they wanted or needed, rather than delivering help that sometimes was at cross purposes or undid what the other group was trying to do.

We had several key advantages:

- The state group with which we worked was incredible; its mission was the kids. The group members were smart and driven people and they were open to new research-based ideas.

- Our group, as a rule, always customizes its approach to the needs of the school rather than making a school conform to a canned program.

- We had air cover, with both district and state officials wanting to see if this model could work.

- We had schools able to quickly overcome the paranoia of state coaches and outside consultants embedded in their schools, and therefore, everyone was able to join in the collaborative spirit.

- We were tasked with helping to create a process that would provide education on state scoring; find out what data we had, needed and wanted; and assist schools in figuring out how to track progress.

We convened with our state counterparts in a modified trailer converted to their offices (this group did not need much office space because they believed they needed to be out in the schools helping). Over the course of a week, we unpacked the state scoring methodology, wrote a manual for helping teachers and leadership understand how they would be graded, and created an easy way to see how a school was doing in any particular category and how the whole school's grade was tracking.

We tried to keep it simple. We only used programs which we knew teachers would have access to like Microsoft Word and PowerPoint. We included all materials they would need in the tool sets developed for our schools. Then, we took everything out to the schools and provided as much professional-development and coaching as the schools needed. To some degree, they were accountable to us (the academic management organization running their institutions) and to the state (which ultimately would be grading the schools), but we approached each school with one theme: Here is our suggestion regarding data collection and usage, but if you have a better way or another methodology fits your needs better, let us help you with it.

Several schools used the data notebook as a resource to look up details on test score calculation or terms in the glossary to see exactly how the state defined an item. Most of our schools used our tracking slides and details on how to set up a school data room. After a month of using the data-tracking protocols and individual and rollup visuals, we moved to the next step, and started having data chats with the teachers. At first, we would crunch the data and share the findings with the teachers on where their classes might need a little extra help, but they wanted us to train them on how they could figure things out for themselves to eliminate some go-between. We could usually take a test or a scrimmage and turn the data around in three to four days, but teachers and instructional coaches wound up wanting to turn it around themselves in one day so that they could feed immediate value back into the class while the assessment was still timely.

The last step was to push this down to the students. This is where the state coach did most of the heavy lifting. She was an expert in helping students make meaning out of the data. She would cover where the students were strong, where they could get the best bang for their buck and let them help determine their course of action. Data chats with students ended up being wildly successful with students understanding more metadata about their learning process than most in the district would have thought possible.

It was important that our team went this route:

- Doing the heavy lifting of unpacking and summarizing the state assessment and accountability documents

- Using this core knowledge to either help schools that were lacking a process or add value to the processes already in place

- Taking as much time to explain the process of data tracking and targeted intervention as needed

- Training the school leaders to track data for the school

- Training the teachers to determine the effectiveness of their strategies in their own classes and pinpointing where student work was breaking down

- The Holy Grail. We worked with students to understand, track, and improve their own performance

---

Data chats with students ended up being wildly successful with students understanding more metadata about their learning process than most in the district would have thought possible.

To some degree, these schools might have remained under the impression they had to do what we told them. We needed outside validation that this worked as well as we thought. Our confirmation came in two phases. First, we found schools that were not assigned to our company or the state intervention team using our specifications. A friend and colleague forwarded copies of the materials, and these schools were able to use the explanations, samples, and instructions to create a schoolwide tracking system that drilled down to an individual student's performance without actually attending our professional-development sessions or having us there to get them started. We were thrilled.

Our second confirmation came when many of the schools
we'd worked with that year came off the state intervention list. This
meant that they either greatly reduced state and outside consulting
resources or, in some cases, shed them altogether. Because we
became close with many of the curriculum coaches and teachers,
we continued to check in on them from time to time. Not only did
they continue to use the system we'd put together, but in many cases,
they built on it and made it their own. Because they understood the
fundamentals of tracking school and student data — and because no
one knows a school better than the leadership team and the teachers
who are there every day — they built homegrown additions to their
data rooms to track the specific school initiatives on which they
were focusing.

There are two issues many districts face, though. First, there is often
no understanding of the real usefulness of data. Second, it is difficult
for an outsider to implement a one-size-fits-all, fidelity-to-the-model
system that doesn't cater to the individual school. This year of
collaboration among the consulting company, school, district, and
state proved the concept that if we work backward from what bene-
fits the student, different entities can work together to help struggling schools as a whole. Turf battles and canned programs rarely
provide a real solution to school issues. They are, at best, partially
or unintentionally successful. At worst, they can do harm to an
already-struggling school.

Our approach now gives us the ability to work in-depth on red flags
as they arise. We can closely define our data points, assess for cause,
make a plan to remediate the cause, and monitor the quality of the
plan's implementation and impact on those areas where we wanted
to see impact. One surprise result of this was we could sometimes
improve student performance in a number of ways in addition to

higher test scores. We found test scores were very inefficient in determining progress and sometimes led us to plan based on assumptions rather than analysis of more relevant data.

We don't have one progress-monitoring system we use in all schools; we encourage schools to develop targeted progress-monitoring systems based on the priority elements of their own plans and the priority needs they have identified in their own students. We encourage them to envision what their school would look like if the plan worked successfully for their students. We then look at critical areas and develop tools, protocols, and data-collection applications to help monitor those areas. In our workshops and in our literature, we identify several characteristics that we link to effective progress monitoring:

The monitoring needs to be tightly targeted to the school's plan's priorities. While improved test scores are the goal, measuring progress only by these marks will not enable progress. The school must be able to measure progress by effectively addressing the causal factors of low test scores that were identified in the school's planning process.

The monitoring needs to be comprehensive and focus not just on one data point but also on a wide variety of collective and individual data points as well.

The monitoring needs to be linked. Many times, multiple data streams are kept in separate silos and are never pulled together to see if there's a bigger picture not seen in individual data sets. If we can't link student progress to student learning work in the classroom and to the school culture and climate, we find it difficult to build plans getting us beyond the Band-Aid stage of school improvement.

The monitoring needs to be current. Iteration loops must be tight. Data from last year are *fossil records*, and data from last month are *antiques*. Our data must inform us of what our status is *today*.

Currently, when we go into a school needing assistance, we are confident we can help the school decide what student proficiency looks like, set realistic goals, develop strategic plans for reaching those goals, and create a monitoring system that will enable the school to measure progress in the areas critical to its plan. We believe this is a major key to moving away from Band-Aid solutions, which may provide a bump in scores but do not change practice systemically.

When we started working with turnaround schools, we used progress-monitoring strategies that really prohibited progress monitoring. We used scores and disaggregated groupings and relied on assumptions about what those scores and groupings meant to making academic-planning decisions and student support program decisions in a very accidental fashion. As we evolved our progress monitoring, we relied less and less on assumptions and more and more on data streams that really defined the current level of performance of each of our students and informed our academic interventions as it supported decision making. As a result, we were able to develop plans that actually could be monitored at the student-impact level and were much more successful in moving all students from where they were to where they were supposed to be by the time they took the test or made their transitions to the next level.

PRACTITIONER'S NOTE

In the tool kit, we have included a classroom observation tool, a student work analysis checklist, a teacher work analysis checklist, and a data management self-assessment.

CLASSROOM OBSERVATION TOOL

Room #: _____   Grade: _____   Teacher: _____

Date: _____   Start time: _____   End time: _____

Subject: _____   Topic: _____   Observer: _____

	Teacher Work	Student Work	Student Engagement
5 mins			
10 mins			

	Teacher Work	Student Work	Student Engagement
15 mins			
20 mins			
25 mins			
30 mins			

STUDENT WORK ANALYSIS

Student: **Class:**   **Date:**   **Test Score:**

Task/Content	Purpose	Execution	Quality	Impact
	• Acquire • Practice • Translate • Create meaning • Equivalent experience	• Followed directions/completed • Followed but not completed • Did not follow or complete • Did not attempt	• Consistent high quality • Mix high and adequate • Adequate • Mix adequate and inadequate • Inadequate	• All related items correct • Most related items correct • Missed most related items • Missed all related items • No effort on test
	• Acquire • Practice • Translate • Create meaning • Equivalent experience	• Followed directions/completed • Followed but not completed • Did not follow or complete • Did not attempt	• Consistent high quality • Mix high and adequate • Adequate • Mix adequate and inadequate • Inadequate	• All related items correct • Most related items correct • Missed most related items • Missed all related items • No effort on test
	• Acquire • Practice • Translate • Create meaning • Equivalent experience	• Followed directions/completed • Followed but not completed • Did not follow or complete • Did not attempt	• Consistent high quality • Mix high and adequate • Adequate • Mix adequate and inadequate • Inadequate	• All related items correct • Most related items correct • Missed most related items • Missed all related items • No effort on test

TEACHER WORK ANALYSIS

Design	Execution	Quality	Impact
• Related to test expectations • Focused on student performance expected • Various materials and technologies • Various methods of delivery • Differentiated student work • Effective work set included • Design of engagement plan • Checks for learning planned	• Lesson plan, critical learnings and materials ready • Teacher started class promptly and made smooth transitions • Academic rituals in place and effective • Teacher kept all students highly engaged in work • Teacher kept most students highly engaged in work • Student engagement was monitored, and corrective feedback given	• High quality student and teacher work • Mix high quality and adequate teacher and student work • Adequate student and teacher work • Mix adequate teacher work and inadequate student work • Both inadequate	• 80% got all related items correct • 80% got most related items correct • 80% got about 1/2 related items correct • 80% missed most related items • 80% missed all related items • 80% gave no effort on related questions

DATA MANAGEMENT SELF-ASSESSMENT

Indicator	Rating		
Our school data plan was designed with best practices in mind.	1	5	10
The school identified the performance expected of all students and identified the data streams needed to monitor and support those expectations.	1	5	10
The school acquired the technology and established the information management systems needed to capture the critical data elements.	1	5	10
Teachers are surveyed regularly to determine if data systems are adequate to their needs.	1	5	10
The school's data management system (DMS) is advanced enough to allow ad hoc queries and capture of data stored in separate subsystems.	1	5	10
The DMS was streamlined to facilitate daily entry and retrieval by teachers and administrators.	1	5	10
The DMS allows easy and timely transmission of data among role groups.	1	5	10
Use of the data management system is regularly monitored and evaluated to determine frequency and impact of use.	1	5	10
The school's DMS generates, collects, and organizes data needed to evaluate the success, or lack thereof, of schoolwide/districtwide initiatives.	1	5	10
The school's data management system allows the tracking/assisting of both individual students and targeted groups.	1	5	10
The school data system enables teachers to relate/pattern the relationship between teacher work, student work, and student performance.	1	5	10
Teachers were trained and provided with the resources needed to use data management systems effectively.	1	5	10

Key: *1–3 Area of Major Weakness, 4–7 Minimally Acceptable, 8–10 Area of Best Practice*

Indicator	Rating		
The data is analyzed and shared by multiple role groups.	1	5	10
The school uses data to identify or evaluate intervention strategies, materials, and plan priorities.	1	5	10
All plans incorporate and are based on current student-performance data.	1	5	10
The school meets proposed national standards for data management (e.g., levels of security, accuracy, ease of collection/retrieval, flexibility).	1	5	10
The school's data management plan was designed and supported with an end (see #2) in mind and is adjusted/expanded as needed.	1	5	10
Key: 1–3 Area of Major Weakness, 4–7 Minimally Acceptable, 8–10 Area of Best Practice			

Notes:

_____

_____

_____

_____

_____

_____

_____

_____

_____

_____

_____

_____

_____

_____

_____

_____

_____

_____

_____

_____

_____

_____

_____

_____

_____

_____

06

I'VE GOT A PLAN

Before we began Ed Directions, planning was something we thought we did well. We used data, identified problems, and made plans to solve the problems. We used terms like *powerful* and *cutting edge* and created plans passing everyone's rubric. Unfortunately, few of our plans improved the performance of underperforming students.

When we started working with schools as education consultants, many of us reflected on the lack of success with underperforming students and tried to figure out what was wrong with the plans. The first thing we noticed was the goal of our plan was to have a plan that sounded good. We included data on students and test scores because they helped the plan sound relevant. We followed a strategic planning model because it ensured we would meet the criteria included in the planning rubric. Most of our plans were designed to change adult behaviors. When we monitored our plans, we checked if the adults were doing what they were supposed to do. When the results came out, we were surprised that, although the adults did the things they were supposed to do, students did not improve.

When we went into schools, we found that most of them had a plan before we visited. Many plans were made in February long before the year's test results were back, and in fact, before the students had even taken the test. Schools made plans and budgets without knowing what they had to do when they had to do it, or how they could tell if it was getting done. We found that because of state and district mandates, changing the way schools planned was a daunting proposition. Many times, we were forced to make a plan based on student-performance data that was two years old by the time the plan was implemented. We knew that this was an ineffective way to build a plan and worked for several years to identify a planning process that would actually enable schools to change student performance in an intentional fashion.

Today we have a planning protocol we follow that includes the following:

- The development of specific, quantifiable, observable goals for improving student learning and performance.

- The development of strategic, logistic, and tactical plans that will enable all staff to work toward the implementation of the school plans.

- Sufficient budget, time, and personnel to make sure all the parts of the plan can be implemented.

- A plan for monitoring implementation and impact on student performance.

- A time schedule for evaluating the plan to see if it's working and to make adjustments if it's not working as advertised. (Plans should always reflect the most current student-performance data available.)

- A schedule for evaluating each stage in the school year to deter-mine if things can be done better next year and to begin planning for next year before the lessons learned are lost.

- A structure integrating school-strategic and tactical planning with teacher course, unit, and lesson planning.

For the protocol to work as an effective part of school change, we found that we had to change mindsets in school leadership and especially in district staff. We had to get them to change precon-ceived notions of what planning best practice was. Leaders had to understand the strategic and tactical planning process and how that linked to instruction and learning in their building. They had to be managers of the plan and leaders of instructors — a process that required an understanding of student-focused planning and the importance of both strategic and tactical plans. If leaders did not understand the rhythm of the learner year, how students learn, or what factors determine the level at which students will perform, they could not develop plans that actually focused on improving student performance over time.

For the instructional staff, there are a number of issues that have to be brought into play in planning for learning. In many cases, we find that we have teachers who don't understand what the standards require — they have never unpacked the standards completely — who have never heard of the five-legged model or the competencies needed for successful transitions, and who have never really tried to identify causal elements of performance or made plans to address causes rather than content. Without these understandings, teachers can't develop lessons that move all students toward standards expectations, monitor their progress toward those expectations, or provide targeted assistance when progress is not adequate. Without an understanding of the rhythm of the learner year and how students learn, teachers can't plan lessons to make all students learners and to build student work in the various periods of the student year to increase both the rigor and level of engagement in classroom work.

In most schools, we revisit the PD plan and suggest that a new round of PD is needed to facilitate teacher movement from teacher-focused lessons to lessons built around learner work. Most times, schools are reluctant to try to change plans because of the procedures involved (the tail wags the dog). Sometimes they are even forbidden to change the plan without board or state approval. It makes it very difficult when schools are committed to implementing a plan that doesn't work and disciplined if they try to change it. To change a school, there has to be a plan and it has to relate to the students who are in the building and what they need to do to become more proficient performers. This usually means that we develop an action plan outside the school plan.

Most school plans we encounter are directed at the adults in the building, not the students. It is as though, at some point in the planning process, someone said, "OK, team, we can see what's wrong: *Our* scores in (name a subject) are low. Now, what does our school leadership team as well as the faculty, as a whole, have to do to get these scores up?" In some ways, this is only natural. Educators take their school's scores very seriously. They own them and feel responsible for them, and they desperately want to improve them. A school planning committee can start with the right idea — a statement of need in student-performance terms — and, as though unconscious, design a plan that targets the adults. We realized, early on, this was a major challenge we would need to address directly.

AN EXAMPLE OF A TYPICAL INPUT/ACCIDENTAL SCHOOL-PLAN COMPONENT

Goal: increase percentage of students who are proficient and increase the number of students who make gains, including students in the bottom quartile on all state assessments

---

Most school plans we encounter are directed at the adults in the building, not the students.

Problem: teacher implementation of the gradual release model is inconsistent.

To-Dos:

- Schools provide schoolwide professional development to correct implementation of gradual-release model.

- Conduct informal/formal observations to discover if teachers are releasing students to practice/investigate on their own. Look at lesson plans to see if gradual release is being planned into lessons and is implemented.

- Administrators check or review coaches' logs for evidence of coaching cycle being implemented.

- Academic coaches implement coaching cycle with teachers by modeling lessons in the classroom.

- Conduct walk-throughs and informal/formal observations to observe implementation of gradual release after coaching cycle is complete.

- Allow teachers the opportunity for purposeful observation of model classroom.

At some point in the needs-assessment process, this sample school assumed low scores are, in part, the result of the teachers not conducting gradual release effectively. Gradual release is a part of any good lesson sequence and design. After all, testing requires independent performance and it pays to emphasize any strategy that will help develop student independence.

Would this gradual release model improve student performance? Moreover, how would you know if it did? Do you know exactly what the students do when released or if there is any pattern to the types of problems their work exhibits? Are there specific objectives or outcomes that gradual release is supposed to develop in students?

The problem with this model is that it is developed with a focus on the adult side of the problem, and all the activities focus on changing the adult behaviors. That means the student side is not addressed. The work and experience set provided for students may or may not address any identified priority need of any student. In terms of the student side, it is an accidental plan. At the end of the implementation process, the only thing the school leaders would know was which teachers implemented the gradual-release model and which did not. They would have no evidence that related to how the gradual-release model affected the work students did in class or their performance on assessment. Compare the language and activities of the adult-focused plan with those included in a sample student-focused plan.

AN OUTPUT/INTENTIONAL PLANNING COMPONENT

Problem: When released from teacher/classroom supports/scaffolding to do an activity independently, 55 percent of the students are unable to articulate and follow the directions for the activity.

As the problem is framed here, it is the students who have the problem, not the teachers. The teachers now have something specific to fix: student understanding of and attention to the directions of a task. Improvement can be measured as students are released to independence and would leverage scores on assessments.

The following solutions are designed accordingly. Note how long it takes before an adult becomes the problem for the administrator.

When released from teacher/classroom supports/scaffolding to do an activity independently, 55 percent of the students are unable to articulate and follow the directions for the activity.

To-Dos:

- Make the 55 percent number real by identifying the students and distributing class lists accordingly.

- Collect learning work and performance samples at the level of state assessment from these students and analyze in biweekly grade-level PLCs for improvement and ongoing issues. Strategies and tactics to address these issues will be developed for implementation in the classrooms.

- The coaching cycle will evaluate the effectiveness of the strategies and tactics developed at these PLCs through observations of students working independently.

- Subsequent work samples will be collected to monitor implementation, impact, and progress. The coaching cycle will evaluate the effectiveness of the strategies employed through observations of students working independently.

- Students who continue to have difficulty with independent work at the assessment level will receive targeted RTI support at the tier II and III levels, as needed.

- Administrators will lead PLC meetings; evaluate the impact of implementation through classroom observation, analysis of student work, and progress on formative and summative assessments; and conference individual teachers where progress is less than satisfactory.

This model focuses on which students need to be changed, how they need to be changed, and what's going to be done to change them. It sets up targeted support for students who still struggle and provides for targeted RTI monitoring as the process moves forward. This intentional planning (as opposed to accidental) is very tightly and precisely focused on students, their needs, and the plan to address their needs.

In a world of high-stakes accountability, accidental plans are risky. Accidental plans are a gamble that strategies implemented will improve student scores. Intentional plans identify what needs to be done to improve student scores and make sure the improvement happens in a timely fashion with intentional results. As turnaround agents, we have found it is difficult to turn around a school with an accidental plan.

PRACTITIONER'S NOTE

Planning is a critical issue in schools. We found that many plans are outdated before they are even finished. The tools for chapter 6 include: a checklist to see if the school has really enabled the plan to be successful, a teacher translation activity, and the systems self-assessment for planning.

SCHOOL PLAN ENABLING CHECKLIST

Critical Questions	Status	Next Steps
Have we identified and examined all needed data?		
Are our objectives clear and student focused?		
Do we have tactical action plans from all staff?		
Have we had adequate training?		
Have we located needed human resources?		
Are our materials adequate?		

Status Key: (1) absolutely under control, (2) working on it, (3) just heard of it and planning and (4) never thought about it.

Critical Questions	Status	Next Steps
Is our technology adequate?		
Will our policies and systems support change?		
Have we provided the time needed to ensure success?		
Has adequate space been allocated?		
Is our evaluation plan adequate?		
Are there other resources that are necessary for success?		
Have we planned to get buy in and engagement from all role groups?		

Status Key: (1) absolutely under control, (2) working on it, (3) just heard of it and planning and (4) never thought about it.

TEACHER TACTICAL PLAN

1. What parts of the school plan require change(s) in my job/classroom?

_____

_____

_____

_____

_____

_____

2. What will be my top priority?

_____

_____

_____

_____

_____

_____

3. What specific plan activities will I implement, and when will they be completed?

_____

_____

_____

_____

_____

_____

4. What is the expected impact on my students' work/performance?

_____

_____

_____

_____

_____

_____

5. To be successful, I will need ...

_____

_____

_____

_____

_____

_____

TEACHER TRANSLATION ACTIVITY

Action Item	Start	End	Person in Charge	Evaluation Activities

PLANNING SELF-ASSESSMENT

Indicator	Rating		
Our school culture was designed with best practices in mind.	1	5	10
The school's planning process is inclusive. All role groups are provided with access and encouraged to participate. **(Inclusive)**	1	5	10
Planning is student focused and driven by the school's success in moving all students to expected levels of performance. **(Student-Focused)**	1	5	10
The planning process begins with analysis of data (scores, structural and causal analysis, and noncognitive indicators). **(Data-Driven)**	1	5	10
The plan establishes specific student-performance goals as the purpose for planning. **(Proactive)**	1	5	10
Analysis of data trends supports a search for relevant best practices. **(Research-Based)**	1	5	10
Action plans are developed to establish how and when goals will be reached. Activities relate directly to improvement goals. **(Consistent)**	1	5	10
A time/task calendar is established to define expected completion dates and individual responsibilities. **(Scheduled)**	1	5	10
All action plans include enabling, implementing, and evaluating plans to encourage successful implementation. **(Implementable)**	1	5	10
The plan includes regular monitoring, review, and revision. It allows and encourages adjustment as needed. **(Flexible)**	1	5	10
The plan is published and communicated to all stakeholders. Parents and students are aware of critical plan elements. **(Known)**	1	5	10
The plan is read by all staff/stakeholders and translated into personal action (tactical) plans. **(Translated)**	1	5	10
Planning is ongoing. Review and evaluation initiate the next planning cycle. **(Continuous)**	1	5	10

Key: 1–3 Area of Major Weakness, 4–7 Minimally Acceptable, 8–10 Area of Best Practice

Notes:

_____

_____

_____

_____

_____

_____

_____

_____

_____

_____

_____

_____

_____

_____

_____

_____

_____

_____

_____

_____

_____

_____

_____

_____

_____

07

REDEFINING BEST PRACTICE: WHAT TO DO WHEN BEST PRACTICE IS NOT ENOUGH

When Ed Directions started consulting outside the Commonwealth of Kentucky, the company leadership spent several days discussing whether the practices we were using would be best practices in other states. Our conclusion was that, because we did not have one product or program, we were marketing as best practice and were, in fact, delivering an approach to school turnaround rather than a program for turning around a school that most of what we did would be transferable. We were almost correct; the approach worked, but we found we had to change language and schedules based on differing state procedures and protocols. When we went to our first new state, we were able to point out that we didn't have a program to sell them, but we would try to help them identify what their students had to do and help them prepare to help students do it at the level required.

This seemed to make sense to the educators in the new states, and it became a part of our corporate culture.

Unfortunately, many of the preconceptions we discussed still exist in the world of turnaround work and education today. One of these is the idea of classroom best practice. There's a whole cottage industry in education for best practices. These practices consist of strategies, techniques, methodologies, and the like to produce changes in teaching and possibly learning. They are called *research-based* if their effects were proven statistically significant across a number of applications in real-world settings and studies.

For the most part, these ideas were accepted as *best practices*. When we experimented with them in classrooms, we found they worked for some students but didn't investigate why they didn't work with other students. We assumed the other students failed to learn the material and this mindset shaped a large number of our early intervention strategies. Some of those strategies are as follows:

- Curriculum-development best practice called for a standards-based design for the further enhancement of the curriculum. States and national organizations developed standards-based curriculum frameworks, and districts fleshed those out into curriculum maps and pacing guides on which teachers were trained to develop standards-based units and lessons. Schools were given one-size-fits-all unit and lesson plans, and nontraditional and underperforming students were ground up in the process.

- Classrooms were required to have visible references to the standard being taught. These were usually written on the board often accompanied by a list of critical knowledge or guiding questions. High-level questions, differentiated activities, thinking activities, engaging activities, and beginning and ending class rituals were assumed to be included in the lesson activities but were rarely included intentionally.

- Sociocultural differences must be addressed, and the education vendors and gurus provided strategies for specific socio-economic, ethnic, and racial groups. Not only were teachers to differentiate for learning style and learning rate, but they needed to differentiate for the sociocultural groups as well.

- Many districts purchased lesson plans advertised as rigorous applications designed to have all students working at high levels. In many cases, strict fidelity to a model was expected when teaching these programs, and teacher inconsistency was considered problematic. Many vendors attributed student failure to a lack of fidelity to the model and blamed the teacher.

- All strategies in school improvement plans had to be seen as *research-based*, even if the research was unrelated to the population of the school or to the learning and performing problems shared by students there. In many cases, this caused schools that identified priority student needs through action research to purchase programs that were unrelated to their real student needs.

- Classroom observations required a focus on what the teacher did in class and whether he or she followed the steps of the adopted methods or strategies. Fidelity to implementation was strictly monitored so that all teachers were expected to be on the same page or activity on the same day.

As long as we held on to this mindset of how to approach school interventions, we tended to be very teacher-focused. The teachers were required to use the best practices specified in the school plan.

If there were students who did not show progress after engaging in the practices, it was assumed that the teacher failed to implement the activity with fidelity.

To be fair, the adoption and implementation of many of these practices were improvements from what was previously in place. Anytime we can replace ineffective practices with better ones, students benefit. However, it is a mistake for schools to adopt them as if they are *silver bullets* to solve the school's central problems.

Anytime we can replace ineffective practices with better ones, students benefit.

This point was driven home to us countless times early on; one of our major *aha* moments came during our first year in the field. We went into a large high school that had reading scores in the single digits — bad. Our immediate thought was to go to our tool kit and select a few research-based reading programs for the school to use to get their state scores up. When we conducted an inventory, we found that the school was using 13 different research-based reading texts and programs and still had reading scores in the single digits.

It isn't hard to imagine the difficulties of managing so many different sets of materials and independent approaches. In this case though, there was not even an attempt to manage them. The administrators were fine with the situation because each program had the best practice seal of approval, which was the same reason the central office had approved the purchases. The teachers were OK with the situation because they used what they wanted from the available options.

Everybody had an excuse for why the scores remained in the single digits — yet still the kids could not read.

When we approached some of the 13 vendors who had each sold the school a different reading strategy, they consistently responded that the teachers must not be implementing their programs with fidelity. This presented a major problem because the reading teachers in the school were trained and deemed best-practice practitioners by the vendors and were thus qualified to train other teachers in the district. The very same vendors then assumed those teachers weren't implementing with fidelity, so something else must be wrong.

> *When we approached some of the 13 vendors who had each sold the school a different reading strategy, they consistently responded that the teachers must not be implementing their programs with fidelity.*

This caused us to rethink the way we designed and used our school and classroom tool kits. We looked at the state's reading test specifications and released test items to determine what was required for proficiency (as framed by the five-legged model). We interviewed the few proficient students at the school along with many students who were struggling. We found the following:

- To score proficiently, students had to have an attitude empowering them to stick with the reading assignment and respond thoughtfully at the end. They had to be willing to give their best effort to both the reading and the written responses.

- Students' confidence to both read the selection and answer the questions was imperative. If the students believed they would be unsuccessful, they would be.

- Basic reading competency was required because students had to be able to understand the text and move through it with some fluency.

- Students had to more fully comprehend what they were reading. For instance, students should be able to tell what was meant, inferred, or concluded in the material they were reading.

- Students had to be able to read fast enough to finish selections in the time allocated. On some high-school tests, students had to read at least 300 words a minute to finish the test in the allotted time.

- Students had to have a successful experience reading the type of genre presented in a particular assessment venue.

- Students had to be able to successfully respond to reading in the ways required on an assessment. Sometimes they could read and comprehend the selections but could not answer questions at proficient levels.

- Students had to be proficient in writing. Many questions required students to make statements about what they'd read and support their responses with examples from the text.

Because any of these variables could disqualify a student from being proficient, we decided to give them a reading test to identify the variables that commonly disqualified students at the school. When we started designing the test, we found there wasn't one single test that would determine what we wanted to know, so we put together a battery of reading assessments.

In addition, we had teachers observe students as they took the test and identify the students who lost attention, didn't give a best effort, or seemed to give up on their exam. Afterward, we interviewed focus groups of students, and at the end of the process, we found the biggest issues were attitude, confidence, higher-level comprehension, reading speed, and question-type experience.

When we examined our findings in the context of the 13 reading programs in place in the school, we found the following:

- None of the 13 programs required students to answer constructed-response (written) questions about the reading. Some included short-answer written responses, but these were different in both complexity and length from the questions that would appear on the real test. We were amazed the majority of students in the school had never written a proficient answer to an open-response question about something they had read. In fact, many were never required to answer an open-response question of any kind in class.

- Not one of the programs was specifically designed to build or change attitude. One thing that everybody agreed on was students at the school hated reading, wouldn't read and wouldn't take reading tests seriously. As a result, we had a majority of the students taking a reading test and not giving a best effort. This skewed the results and gave us a false read, leading us to believe the students read at a much lower level than their actual ability.

- More than 75 percent of the students who took our test battery described themselves as poor readers, meaning, again, the score was probably a false read. One of the 13 programs developed student confidence, but this program was only used in one special-education reading class.

- The test battery we gave required students to read about 200 words a minute to finish in the time allotted. Only 10 students *in the school* finished every reading and answered every question in time. The majority of students ran out of time and guessed on the last few questions. This gave us a false read: The issue was pace, but the raw score told us something else.

- One reading was three pages long with no visuals; almost half the students skipped this reading and guessed at the answers. When asked about it, the students said the reading selection was too long for them to read and answer.

- Our questions required thoughtful reading. Many required students to infer, conclude, or apply reasoning based on what they had read. Most of the students were competent word callers, and almost all could determine the literal meaning, but they struggled when responding beyond a literal level. The remedial and support programs purchased by the school focused only on basic reading and literal meaning. While there was some inclusion of higher-level reading and response in some of the literature courses, this usually involved fiction, and the teacher would initiate the thinking process for the class and let the students respond.

We concluded all 13 of these programs were based in research and most were considered best practice by conventional wisdom — but also, and more importantly, they did not meet the needs of the students in this school. If we were going to improve school performance, we had to accept that best practices are not best practices if they have no relevance for the student needs and learning styles in the classroom. There are no best practices without some sort of context.

If we were going to improve school performance, we had to accept that best practices are not best practices if they have no relevance for the student needs and learning styles in the classroom.

Accordingly, we changed our definition of best practice. Best practice starts with the students present in the classroom. It has to be *their* practice, not the teachers' practice, driving classroom planning. Variables in reading proficiency are developed through student work, not through teacher work; if we want to focus on best practices to change student performance, we start by focusing on the work students actually perform.

This school was trying to fix basic reading — a problem that, in this case, did not exist. By doing so, they doomed themselves to single-digit scores.

BEST PRACTICE AS IT RELATES TO STUDENT WORK

As our work continued, we understood there are some key areas of student work that help determine whether a particular work activity is a best practice for students.

- Student work must recognize the learning process as a critical element for acquiring new learning. Students must acquire new learning, organize it for memory, create meaning for it, and use it in ways that are equivalent, in language complexity and length, to any official assessments administered on the knowledge.

- Differentiation needs to move away from ritual differentiation (differentiating for the sake of differentiating irrespective of the exact learning needs in a particular class) and provide for differentiated work based on student need (e.g., differentiating for learning rate, acquiring preference, organizing preference, thinking level, and perceptions of self as learner).

- Student work needs to change as we move through the school year. Student work appropriate for the beginning of the year is no longer sufficient the month before the test. The needs of a student as a worker frequently change as the learner year progresses.

- Both the teachers and students must be aware of the expected levels of knowledge and performance. Teacher and student work must be intentional in moving the students from where they are to where they need to be. Accidental development of the student can cause that student to miss the development of a critical characteristic and fail to answer questions correctly when he or she knows the answer.

- Student and teacher work must be congruent in language, task, rigor, venue, and thinking as it pertains to the expectations of the assessment. That is the first step toward what we call intentionality.

- Remediation and support are only best practice when they remediate and support the identified priority needs of individuals or groups of students. Many best-practice remediation programs solve the wrong problem, solve a problem that doesn't exist, or solve a problem that is not a priority need of any of the students being supported.

For these reasons, none of us go into a school with a set program of interventions. Instead, we go in with a series of questions that we would like to have answers to before we suggest solutions. Our data should indicate that we should use it. If it does not, we will end up wasting time and resources by using it.

We believe the following:

- **There is no such thing as best practice unless it is an appropriate strategy for moving the students from where they are to where we need them to be**. We are not saying something marketed as best practice won't be useful — but there's no guarantee, and a product or practice should be used intentionally, not accidentally.

- **Best practice cannot be identified as a teacher-work strategy unless it corresponds to the needs of the appropriate work experience for the student.**

- **Best practice is not just a content-base or knowledge-base issue**. Best practice develops the *other* proficiency characteristics that are required for a student to perform well on an assessment or to make a successful transition to another level. When we talk about the whole learner, this is what we have to mean.

- **Best practice can differ from one part of the year to another part and must be consistent with the learner needs in the learner year**, not the administrative year.

- **Best practice can differ from school to school and from class to class.** We must treat schools and classes as unique individuals. Many times, even schools located in close proximity to one another will have different needs and require different turnaround plans.

Today we start our work in a school by explaining that, for us, best practice is determined by what the students need to be successful. We emphasize an approach to determining best practice rather than a program or a set of materials. This approach requires instructional leaders and teachers to do the following:

- Understand how standards change what we need to do in schools. Standards are for everybody. They do not represent an impossible goal only the gifted can reach. Rather, they are minimal competencies expected of every student in a school.

- Administrators have to understand instructional leadership as well as systems management. Intentionally building learners and performers requires effective systems but also effective instructional leadership.

- Teachers have to understand their job is not to deliver content but to prepare students to meet exit expectations. Redefining the role and purpose as a teacher leads to better, more student-focused plans, better data management, and more learner-focused classrooms.

- Know your students. Before school starts, teachers need to know and understand which students were successful and which ones were not. They need to know the cognitive and noncognitive issues that keep a student from reaching his or her potential.

- Understand the rhythm of the learner year. Student work needs to change in nature and rigor from the beginning of school to the time of the state test.

- The way students learn must be honored in terms of the work students do in classrooms and the types of support they receive outside class.

- Accept that teacher- and school-constructed tests need to prepare students for the different formats and venues they will experience on the state assessments.

- Assistance programs need to be targeted to individual student-priority needs. Students can't be grouped by score or by label but should be grouped by priority need for support programs to work as planned. Anything else is accidental intervention.

- Monitoring cannot be done by merely checking scores. Teachers and PLC groups need to have student performance work and the learning work that preceded the performance in hand to discuss what happened and what they need to do next.

- School leaders must assume responsibility for enabling effective teaching and learning. They should be prepared to change plans, class lists, materials, programs, and so on if results indicate students are not making progress.

- School leaders must assume responsibility for getting students into the classrooms where they will learn. Distributing nontraditional learners or those with behavior problems equally among teachers may not be what's best for students. Nontraditional learners and those with behavior problems need to be with teachers who can transform them into learners and performers.

- Everything is on the table. The plan, the schedule, the program, etc. are not untouchable and have to be changed if they're getting in the way of student progress. They are the tails in this game. Student performance is the dog, and the tail should not wag the dog.

Today each of our coaches has a tool kit, a menu of questions, and data tools used to begin discussions about what a school has to do. Discussions with school staff can indicate whether any of the items in the menu were tried before in the school or if school staff believes an approach might not be productive. Our tool kit is designed to begin discussions, not to be a recipe of best practice activities everyone must follow. Our goal is for school staff to develop the capacity to assess their students' needs and locate interventions that will enable them to meet those needs.

This provides us with a number of advantages in dealing with schools in almost any state.

- We don't have to play *a blame game.* We can focus on a performance issue, diagnose the performance issue, and decide on a prescriptive course of action. The consultants don't have to point a finger at anybody; they can be a part of a solution team with the school staff.

- It allows us to focus school attention on the school's intervention plans and decide if they've collected enough data to inform those plans. We can look at their intervention plan and decide if it is likely to impact the priority student needs that we identified in our first data search.

- It encourages schools to build their own capacity for action research. If they identify a causal issue in student performance and they have nobody on staff who knows how to address that causal issue, they can develop an action research approach that can create in-school experts who can find solutions and address the particular problem at hand.

- It gives the school staff the power to determine best practice. Instead of listening to somebody at a conference who says something is best practice, teachers can look at their students' performance issues, identify a menu of possible solutions, pick one that is appropriate, implement it, and monitor to see if the intervention is having the expected impact.

- It changes the nature of PLC discussions because it enables teachers to look at the performance issues and their interventions and the actual products produced by students to see if the impact on product is what the teachers wanted.

- It can change the nature of administrator/teacher conferences. If teachers are asked about performance issues, and they explain what they're doing, why they're doing it, and how it impacts students, the conference can truly be formative and proactive.

- At Ed Directions, we feel we've developed a protocol for improving learning and performing. This protocol requires better, intentional leadership and instruction. If a school's focus is on building student competencies, it should provide affective curricula, better data management, and more targeted support systems. Schools have to have a best-practice approach to selecting what's best for their students to produce competent, proficient learners and performers. This is the responsibility of school staff. The Ed Directions approach focuses on building these capacities in all school staff.

PRACTITIONER'S NOTE

Redefining *best practice* is very difficult with teachers who already think they are the best teacher in the building. It is important that they are willing to change and to take those actions students need them to, so they can become better learners and performers. We included two tools, one focusing on academic rituals and routines that enable student success: an effective learning rituals self-assessment and an instructional self-assessment.

ACADEMIC RITUALS AND ROUTINES CHECKLIST

Ritual	Issue Area	Possible Next Steps	Priority
Active listening			
Note taking			
Translating learning			
Creating meaning			
Reading to learn			
Using discipline language			

Ritual	Issue Area	Possible Next Steps	Priority
Organizing materials			
Writing in response to reading			
Writing in response to thinking			
Revising work to meet a standard			
Critical reading			
Critique in terms of given criteria			

INSTRUCTIONAL SELF-ASSESSMENT

Indicator	Rating		
The school academic program has been designed to prepare all students to work successfully at the levels defined by academic standards.	1	5	10
Teachers have received the training, time, and assistance needed to translate the program into level, course, and unit plans.	1	5	10
Instruction and management strategies are selected to match learning needs and maximize the performance of all students.	1	5	10
Teachers define unit expectations (critical learnings) and design an assessment that will indicate successful mastery of these expectations.	1	5	10
Lessons are designed to move all students from their entry level to the levels defined in the unit plan. Active learning is expected.	1	5	10
Each classroom has a culture that emphasizes high levels of student engagement, student work, and student thinking.	1	5	10
Each classroom is equipped with materials and technologies consistent with the identified needs of students.	1	5	10
Lessons enable all students to do the learning work (acquire, translate, create meaning, apply at expected levels) required for proficiency.	1	5	10
The school academic program has been designed to prepare all students to work successfully at the levels defined by academic standards.	1	5	10
Required student work meets "best practice" standards for quality of design, level of engagement, and quality of the product.	1	5	10
The rhythm of the learner (formative period, calibrating period, assessment period) is addressed in all lesson plans.	1	5	10

Key: *1–3 Area of Major Weakness, 4–7 Minimally Acceptable, 8–10 Area of "Best Practice"*

Indicator	Rating		
All classes have established academic rituals and routines that reduce wasted time and enable all students to be active, engaged learners.	1	5	10
Required student work meets "best practice" standards for quality of design, level of engagement and quality of the product.	1	5	10
The rhythm of the learner (formative period, calibrating period, assessment period) is addressed in all lesson plans.	1	5	10
All classes have established academic rituals and routines that reduce wasted time and enable all students to be active, engaged learners.	1	5	10
Lessons include activities that accommodate differences in acquiring rate and style, learning style and performance preference.	1	5	10
All students participate in lesson activities and high levels of engagement are expected of all.	1	5	10
Lessons include work that "standardizes" student learning and creates a collective understanding of critical learnings.	1	5	10
Teachers and students are focused on critical vocabularies and minimal operational vocabularies.	1	5	10
All students are included. Experience equity is expected. Each student is encouraged to demonstrate learning in his or her preferred mode.	1	5	10
Students write in response to thinking with or thinking about content daily.	1	5	10
Student learning is assessed, and nonstandard learning is corrected immediately.	1	5	10
Homework reflects "best practice" research and is used to shape student performance.	1	5	10
Key: *1–3 Area of Major Weakness, 4–7 Minimally Acceptable, 8–10 Area of "Best Practice"*			

Notes:

08

GENERATING BETTER DATA: THE ACADEMIC REVIEW

One major frustration of working in turnaround schools is that public perception is largely a function of test scores (bad test scores equals a bad school). For years, Ed Directions struggled to dismantle the fallacy that if a school's scores did not improve, the school did not change. The toughest of schools often need several years of foundation-building to pave the way for performance gains. We worked in schools that were making positive changes in climate and culture, classroom tone and even the design of student work, but still had not managed to achieve significant improvements in student scores. Those aforementioned changes deserved attention as well. They were necessary precursors for subsequent improvements. We developed the academic review process to help bring focus to areas of school improvement critical to test scores but not necessarily reflected yet by those scores.

USING ACADEMIC REVIEW DATA TO JUMP-START SCHOOL CHANGE

It can be difficult to know where to start when approaching a new school. This could be a school on an intervention or turnaround list, or it could be a school stuck at a B rating trying to become an A or state blue-ribbon school. The problem is partially logistics. Assessing the culture, climate and teacher/student work patterns and understanding the school data management plan for a classroom can take a number of observations and absorb a tremendous amount of the coach's time. Another problem is the coach quickly becomes invested in his or her school. While a boon in some ways, it becomes increasingly more difficult for the coach to remain objective in observations. When we started working with turnaround schools, we left the issue of determining the starting point to the individual coaches. Through experiential learning, we discovered that an outside team using an observation protocol can jump-start this process and save the coach months of observation time.

To keep with the theme all best practices are contextual and real data sets need to be used to determine a school's specific needs, Ed Directions developed a process called an *academic review* (AR). Today, we tailor the AR to focus on specific curricular areas, systems or culture, and climate. It became an effective tool for starting our turnaround work at the right place.

WHAT IS AN ACADEMIC REVIEW?

An AR is a data-rich, prescriptive data set used to assess a school's readiness for change and identify specific priority areas where the school needs to change to improve. The AR report can be used as a template to monitor the improvement process as well as stimulate tactical and ad hoc plans. In some schools, we conduct two ARs — one early in the year and one closer to testing. The first establishes current practice and identifies areas of change. The second provides data, allowing the school to check to see if the plan changes have taken place and, if so, to what extent. This pre-use or post-use of the AR is effective when schools make major improvements in student performance in the current testing year.

An AR is a data-rich, prescriptive data set used to assess a school's readiness for change and identify specific priority areas where the school needs to change to improve.

In an AR, a group of educators visits a school for a few days to observe and record trends. This is meant to provide an outside, objective perspective and to see if our data and observations align with a school's self-perception of what is (or should be) happening. A school does not get a grade from an AR. Rather, it receives an overview of what team members observed, a breakdown of climate, culture, and teacher and student work in the classroom and ratings for specific academic indicators.

An AR is different from a classic educational audit. While an audit checks for compliance in key areas, an AR looks at culture, student and teacher work, and interview data. It then correlates them with the portion of the learner year in which the school presently finds itself. (For those who conduct two ARs a year, we perform the second AR when the schools are entering the calibrating period and planning for the test-taking window.)

HOW WE CAPTURE RAW DATA SETS

An AR team coordinates a site visit in advance with the leadership team of a school. The AR team includes a captain, who conducts most of the interviews; observers, who visit classrooms, and an administrator, who coordinates the collection of data. The captain interviews all administrators and teachers, a sample of students and parents and, if possible, counselors and support staff. The observers visit classes, collecting data in 15-minute snapshots, which are then loaded into a database. These snapshots are meant to examine schoolwide trends, not to evaluate individual teacher performances.

The interviews, school documentation, classroom snapshots, and observer end-of-day and database reports are aggregated into a single captain's report. This report is submitted to a team of educators that conducts an in-depth review, distills the most important information, and makes conclusions and recommendations that are presented to the school.

The AR team includes a captain, who conducts most of the interviews; observers, who visit classrooms, and an administrator, who coordinates the collection of data.

WHAT TO DO WITH THE ACADEMIC REVIEW FINAL REPORT

The final report for an AR includes a narrative description, a set of comparisons to best practices for the time of year when the review was completed, and a set of recommendations compiled by the Ed Directions senior team. The analysis of the school data and the expectations of the time of year determine, to a great extent, what would be considered best practice and what we would expect students to be doing. Fall ARs are beneficial for *reality-checking* whether schools opened per plan and the year's major initiatives are understood and have been implemented consistently among different role groups within the school (and whether we see evidence of this in the classroom). Spring ARs collect information about what in the school plan was implemented and provides information to complete preparing students for this year's assessment cycle. Fall and spring ARs can help identify PD initiatives that might be needed ASAP or over the summer. The spring AR can also provide data to determine what must be done to prepare for a more effective opening of school the following year.

It's important to note the schools are not expected to just look at the recommendations, select a few, and set about implementing. The ARs are sets of distilled information and corresponding recommendations based on a small window of data capture. The first step for school staffs in using any is to do a reality check or self-assessment to determine if they agree with the data points and the recommendations. In one example, a school received an academic review report that noted that student engagement differed from classroom to classroom and suggested by way of recommendation that the school look into both management and academic rituals and routines. They didn't do a self-assessment but made the assumption their CHAMPS classroom management strategy rituals were not effective and committed to retraining all staff in the use of CHAMPS protocols. The problem was the data points that drove the observation recommendations from the senior team had little to do with student behavior. The following chart is the tool used to assess students' engagement in their academic work. The recommendation said that school rituals and routines needed to be evaluated with a focus on academic rituals and routines that could increase student engagement in learning work.

Student Work	Student Engagement
Task: • Acquiring work • Organizing work • Creating meaning	• All highly engaged • Some highly engaged, the rest moderately engaged • All moderately engaged • Some moderately engaged, the rest complying • All complying • Some complying, the rest not engaged
Task: • Acquiring work • Organizing work • Creating meaning	• All highly engaged • Some highly engaged, the rest moderately engaged • All moderately engaged • Some moderately engaged, the rest complying • All complying • Some complying, the rest not engaged

The school's action was based on faulty assumptions and led them into a plan that would have a negative impact on increasing student engagement in learning work.

A school should not take the report and immediately start acting upon the recommendations. The first step in using the AR final report is to unpack it. Usually, Ed Directions facilitates this unpacking process, provides a number of tools to walk the school through the different parts of the review, and gives the school a chance for reflection and self-assessment. The first part of the tool kit allows team members to list what they disagree with in the report and provides time for the school to reach consensus on the degree to which the data sets represent actual practice in the school. In the second part of the tool kit (an analysis of the recommendations), the report gives a menu of options for the school and relates them to the data points the senior team used to drive the recommendation. Because most schools have multiple issue areas and receive multiple recommendations and most lack the resources to implement all the recommendations in one year, Ed Directions recommends the team select no more than three to five recommendations that they, themselves, identify as their highest leverage or priority options. The third part of the academic review provides time for the Ed Directions coaches to facilitate action planning, so the school can begin developing a strategic plan that has actual potential to impact issue areas that relate to improving student performance.

The academic review is meant to be a positive tool and not a game of "gotcha" or pin-the-blame.

The academic review is meant to be a positive tool and not a game of "gotcha" or pin-the-blame. It provides synthesized data from normally disparate sources. Its purpose is to give the school's principal and core leadership team some objective perspectives, to review what outsiders observed in a few days, and to provide expert help for interpreting the information and making recommendations from those results. The final report is a starting point to determine whether the school is on track with its main foci and whether everyone is interpreting those foci the same way. It is not the decision point. The decision point that drives a school planning process comes from the debriefing discussion and the school's self-assessment and analysis of data that give meaning to the words that are included in the report.

Ed Directions has implemented academic reviews for almost 20 years, and in the process, we made a number of discoveries that have helped us develop our approach to turnaround schools:

- Few people in schools or in the central office have a good idea of what's going on in classrooms, particularly student work. People monitor what the adults do and not whether the students are improving as learners and performers.

- Most school plans are developed without a database of current practice that can define what changes are needed and how those changes could be best implemented.

- Whether the school agrees with the academic review findings or disagrees strongly with them doesn't matter in terms of results. The discussion of the findings — what they mean and what the school needs to do to improve — is the beginning of an intentional, student-focused planning process.

- The academic review is a high-leverage data point for the school coach. It creates a data point that *the school* identified, and *we* need to address. Instead of a critic, the coach can be a member of a solution team.

- While few schools do a follow-up academic review to determine if outsiders see change in school systems and classrooms, we found when we get to do the second review, either at the end of the year or at the beginning of the next year, we can generate celebrations for changes that worked and lists of issues that are still in need of attention. The second AR becomes a stimulus for the next round of planning.

The academic review gave us a chance to change what leaders look for in classrooms. Almost every observation tool we encountered was tied to the evaluation of what the *teacher* was doing, but we needed to focus on the work the *student* was doing. If observed work was not appropriate for the students, congruent to the standard, or connected to the learning process, we felt that it was not effective work, even if the teacher seemed to be doing a good job.

Eventually, we developed a set of observation tools that enabled us to train school leadership to identify the quality and appropriateness of student work. For example, we might focus on the interaction between teacher and learner, seek evidence that learning was taking place for all students and that students were engaged at the appropriate levels, or any other areas we chose to target based on the school's red-flag profile. These could be customized around a limited number of manageable priority needs. With this training, school leaders could do their own data collection to see if the results of the academic review were still observable in classrooms and if plans were being implemented as designed.

The academic review provided a baseline for Ed Directions to use to begin to shape the thinking base and the competency set leaders and teachers took into their respective roles. For everyone in the building, measuring student progress and changing student work (and at times teacher work) became a very critical part of the effort in turning around schools.

Because our chief task was to improve student scores, we needed a process that would enable us to measure progress in building both learners and performers. To accomplish this, we developed a follow-up tool kit for an academic review. This included a set of work-sweep protocols to collect and analyze the work product of the students. If the learning work was not proficient, we could check to see if learning took place, and if not, we could remediate within 24 hours. We developed academic processing observation forms and data collection tools to deal with a situation where the PLC discussions did not identify a cause or clear results. We used these protocols for observing students at work and conferencing with them about their work with some who were at risk, some with attitude or perception problems, and some with unidentified learning or performance issues. The use of these protocols provided the PLC discussions with tightly focused, organized data points that could be related to findings that came up red-flagged in the academic review.

The academic review is a data point to be discussed and analyzed before it becomes a decision point. Once decisions are made, the follow-up interventions and data collection (needed for implementation and impact analysis) can be designed to be intentional in terms of the academic review red flags.

One outcome of our tool and protocol-development process was the emergence of proficient student profiles. By using the five-legged model, noncognitive indicators (e.g., attendance, discipline, identified mental or physical impediments, and so on), the proficient student competency set, and specific content indicators (e.g., reading speed, computation fluency, and so on), we could monitor the development of the different characteristics students needed to reach proficiency on the state or district assessment. This process gives us the opportunity to benchmark student profiles at the beginning of the year and check progress toward proficiency at points along the way.

With the academic review, we can provide a number of different services benefiting schools. We provide outside eyes to describe the teaching and learning practices going on in classrooms. We provide pre-observation and post-observation sets, allowing schools and districts to assess the implementation and impact of priority plans. We provide air cover for administrators and teachers who are working hard to improve student performance but are working with students who have such significant deficits it will take several years of building to get them to a point where they can and will perform to their potential on the state assessment test.

PRACTITIONER'S NOTE

The academic review process is a major development in the ED approach to turning around schools. It provides multiple data points that can be used to baseline teacher and student work or to demonstrate change in teacher or student work. The academic review unpacking worksheet helps educators make sense of the findings of the final report and review meeting.

ACADEMIC REVIEW — ITEMS THAT WE KNOW WE MUST ADDRESS

Academic Review Concern	Data Points Referenced	Changes Needed — School Systems	Changes Needed — Classroom Practice

09

WE'RE ALL ON THE SAME TEAM, RIGHT?

In previous chapters, we explained our approach to turning around low-performing schools. The basic tenets of our efforts to improve schools are easy to understand; however, they often prove very difficult to implement.

We are familiar with much of the *school-change literature.* Our academic bias runs along the sociocultural, qualitative side of the fence; therefore, we contend schools and their districts are complex, human institutions subject to a wide range of irrational social, political, and cultural forces that complicate change efforts.

In this chapter, we discuss the four forces common in schools where we've worked. We keep the discussion general and anonymous; it is not our intention to embarrass or blame anyone. We do, however, want to bring attention to issues superintendents, districts and leadership teams must think critically about and address as they create and facilitate turnaround efforts.

Each of the following issues could be chapters or books in and of themselves. Instead, we have briefly highlighted four in terms of how each issue affected our work and detail the challenges and successes we experienced in encountering them:

- The blame game, negativity, and believing they can

- Problem solving in compliance cultures

- Instructional orthodoxy, curriculum control, and turf battles

- Managing competing initiatives

THE BLAME GAME, NEGATIVITY, AND BELIEVING THEY CAN

"Who's at fault here? Somebody has to be held accountable!"

Finding fault and laying blame is a national pastime, it seems, and nowhere do people play the game with more energy than in school communities. It is *obstacle number 1*, and it must be overcome before any improvement can take place.

Finding fault and laying blame is a national pastime, it seems, and nowhere do people play the game with more energy than in school communities.

In one school where the blame game was paralyzing, we led a discussion to generate at least one positive, proactive step all role groups could support. We arranged a large meeting including staff, parents, and members of the community. The facilitator began the discussion noting the school's 9 percent proficiency score in reading and then asked, "Does anybody feel this is acceptable?"

Of course, they all said no. The facilitator then started discussions about where everyone thought the school should be; the group said 25 percent would be reasonable. As discussion generated lists of ideas for helping to reach the 25 percent, we noticed that there were not any personal criticisms on those lists. We learned that if you cannot get people to agree on where to go, you sometimes start by getting them to agree that they do not want to stay where they are. This shaped our thinking about the blame game from then on.

There is nothing in our group's protocol asking people to accuse others. Instead, we ask them to tell us what the test scores mean, or in some cases, what they think the students could not do on the test. We get them student-focused before starting discussions about action plans. We use similar protocols to prepare for academic reviews and professional-development planning. We establish a working culture for our team at the school, and a student-focused and proactive culture that will encompass what the students have to do better and what we have to do to make that happen.

The proactive approach to problems provides us a tool for defusing morale issues generated by the "What's the use? We're doomed anyway!" mentality. This approach does the following:

- It allows us to plan with intentionality, to move from one place we don't want to be to another we agree we want to be.

- It saves time by forcing the school to think early about the meaning of performance and expected results — the focus points in our approach.

- It gives us a chance to change a reactive school culture or repressive school climate without actually condemning either. In many low-performing institutions, this is a major help.

- It establishes a working relationship for our team focused on results rather than blame. We use desired outcomes as a filter for dialogue and our data discussions; we don't blame anybody for lack of progress. Every discussion is, instead, framed as "What do we do next?" or "If that didn't work, what will work?"

- With a student focus, we can ask a teacher, "Do you know how to do that?" without blaming that teacher for not knowing how to do it. We can offer professional development or coaching support that is targeted to something the teacher identified as a personal need. We don't have to come in and force teachers into PD or academic programs where they have no buy-in or interest.

We learned if we wanted to be effective from the very beginning of our relationship with a turnaround school, we could not condone reactive discussions about who was responsible for the problems. We could not responsibly recommend a knee-jerk dismissal of staff, change of curriculum, or mandated PD and could certainly not come in with answers to problems we did not own.

We now tell schools changing their scores is hard work. We emphasize changing a school is about asking and answering the right questions, and in almost all cases, those questions must be about the present and future — not about something in the past.

We learned if we wanted to be effective from the very beginning of our relationship with a turnaround school, we could not condone reactive discussions about who was responsible for the problems.

PROBLEM SOLVING IN COMPLIANCE CULTURES

Peter Drucker, the management expert, aptly pointed out almost 60 years ago that management is about doing things right while leadership is about doing the right things. All organizations need both in balance and can suffer when management and leadership are out of balance. When you examine a typical business, the relationship between management and leadership is easier to understand because a business has a clear bottom-line goal, which is profit (by the definition of a business). When you examine schools, the relationship between leadership and management is much more complex.

Peter Drucker, the management expert, aptly pointed out almost 60 years ago that management is about doing things right while leadership is about doing the right things.

School management is largely about improving organizational performance. In a school's case, it is about ensuring that the inputs are in place, understood, and supported. (Inputs can be defined as the school's day-to-day operations or the teacher lesson planning or instruction. These are the things the adults do. Output is the student learning and the student performance of that learning.) *School leadership* is much more, though. It is about defining priorities, communicating them compellingly, and managing to complete them successfully. Leadership is about designing the big picture and communicating the "why" and "how" of what is envisioned, whereas management is about working a plan with precision.

Schools can fall off balance easily. If "doing things right" is the mantra, you might find a well-run school with strict expectations for both the adults and the students. Compliance with those expectations is rewarded and noncompliance sanctioned vigorously; orthodoxy governs, and educators are at risk of losing touch with the needs of the students they teach. However, if "doing the right things" is the central influence at a school, one might see an institution where the vision is clear, compelling, and passionately communicated but cannot be realized because of poor management.

We experienced both extremes in our turnaround work. The more difficult to work with is the hypercompliant culture. In previous chapters, we discussed how turning around low-performing schools requires a problem-solving approach that is causal and intentional.

One large district required schools to implement a set of standards that differed from the tested state standards. This presented alignment issues, but the district adamantly held the standards it was using were superior and better for kids. The district was probably right. In higher-performing schools, scores on these district tests were not an issue because those children already had the language and experience base to handle the slight difficulty bump on the test; persistently low-performing schools, in contrast, struggled to make any gains at all.

One brief case in point was when we convinced a few elementary schools to realign their math standards to the state standards and use materials more at the level and rigor of the assessment. We implemented our progress-monitoring approach and instructional support during the year, and the scores spiked significantly; one of the schools had the largest math gains in the state. The principal was invited to the state capital and given an award, but when he got back, he received an e-mail from his superiors forbidding him from using that approach again on penalty of losing his job.

This is an extreme example, yes, but we saw many examples of more subtle pressures applied to school leadership. In districts with a top-down management culture, the expectation to comply with district initiatives is understandably very high. Schools are expected to, quite simply, do what they are told. In districts more inclined toward hypercompliance, these expectations are rigidly enforced.

Programs and curricula are a necessity. However, we argue low-performing schools need to use these structures in more intentional ways, ways that might require a school to deviate from the learning calendar or to augment specialized materials to address a priority need. Without the freedom to instructionally adapt to the unique demands of its students, a turnaround school is unlikely to improve.

Superintendents, their designees and turnaround principals must understand this to lead effectively. They need to be involved and up to date on the identification of these schools' priority needs in order to promote the right things. They, too, must do the turnaround work we described in previous chapters.

INSTRUCTIONAL ORTHODOXY, CURRICULUM CONTROL, AND TURF BATTLES

Differing philosophies, theories, and views shaped the instructional landscape for years. Battles over whole-language versus direct instruction in reading, concept-based versus traditional skills-based approaches in math and writing as a process versus grammar and style in writing are three of the most contentious. In many respects, they are competing orthodoxies; the true believers defend and attack to protect their perception of what "school improvement" and being a "good school" mean.

In districts, true believers are likely to be found in departments of curriculum and instructional design. They do lots of good work, to be sure, yet we have found they can be very turf-conscious as well, and depending on their levels of influence, they can be significant blockers to turnaround efforts.

One of the first things we do in a new district is try to get a *lay of the land* in terms of these competing pedagogies. While we may have individual preferences as to efficacy, we withhold judgment because our causal, intentional approach is likely to upset the true believers on all sides.

Here is a further example. We worked in low-performing elementary schools in a district scoring consistently poor in writing. When this subject was tested in grade 4, we found the writing experiences of students in grades K–3 were limited, as the schools devoted the majority of instructional time and attention to reading and math. Students came to fourth grade with little or no experience with the on-demand writing of the state assessment. They also came with limited language and sentence sense.

To adequately prepare these fourth graders for the assessment, we deviated from the orthodox (writer's workshop, genre-based) approach of the district and focused more aggressively on language development and on-demand writing. This met a great backlash from true believers, who, we found out, were represented in more places than just the curriculum and instruction unit.

Still, we began to see results immediately, and on that year's assessment, many of these schools scored at or above the district average. Without an external change agent on site, it is doubtful anyone would have effectively challenged the district writing program. We were also fortunate that the turnaround chief assigned to these schools provided the necessary air cover for the schools to make the adaptations, giving us time to initiate and implement interventions that would lead to systemic change.

Low-performing schools need air cover and advocacy when they have to go up against the entrenched orthodoxy. Districts have critical need for a strong curriculum and instruction foundation. In terms of turnaround work, the district leadership needs to make sure its instructional support people involved in the turnaround work sufficiently to understand the stakes in play. We find that when this happens, turf issues are minimized, and the lessons learned from such collaborations go on to strengthen the district's instructional program as a whole.

MANAGING COMPETING INITIATIVES

As a new principal of a turnaround school, one of the authors received a visit from a central office support person in November who asked how the parent-in-prison program was going. That's how, after four months on the job, the principal learned the school even *had* a parent-in-prison program. To complicate matters, the principal learned that the city's most vocal and contentious community leader — someone who either could be a great help or a great threat to him — had coordinated the program.

The point is turnaround principals must be on top of so many initiatives and able to manage such abundances of help. These sources of help may be well-intentioned, useful, and good for the kids — though we saw principals run ragged trying to satisfy the needs and demands of too many misaligned resources. In some cases, these demands take attention away from the turnaround work they must lead first to improve the school. In other cases, ostensibly helpful programs can actually be a barrier to making progress if implemented poorly or haphazardly.

The same can be said of superintendents who can be helpful or can impede progress. In one small district, for example, we had a two-year contract to work with three middle and two high schools. We enjoyed the full support of district leadership, including the superintendent, and we were able to help the schools focus on needs more intentionally. It was some of our most rewarding work; all five schools showed impressive gains after that first year.

The next year was very different. The superintendent was given the opportunity to receive, free-of-charge, a team of state support professionals assigned to his district full time. While we were still under contract, it quickly became apparent to us that the superintendent had shifted his attention to the state-assistance team as, politically, he should have.

While we found ways to accommodate the new direction, it took away most of the time and resources we had available for professional learning communities and professional-development work. The momentum established around student work stopped and was replaced by a mandatory alignment project involving the participation of every teacher and staff member in the district. That shift hurt staff morale as well; the momentum that the increase in scores created was visibly short-lived, and a compliance attitude settled in.

Such is the vulnerability of the outside agent; we understood that going in. The same dynamic repeats itself no matter who is involved; either multiple initiatives begin at the same time or one starts, only to be run over by the next one. Principals in turnaround schools often end up with too many masters to serve. If school leadership and faculty have been around for a number of years, they can easily develop an attitude that sounds like "this too shall pass" and may try to play out the clock on an initiative.

School and district leaders need to understand the nature of turn-around work and, especially, how it must be protected from the goal distortion and displacement that come from managing multiple separate initiatives if they are to guard against this.

We explained our approach to what turnaround work should look like and how it should be implemented. The obstacles to it, outlined here, could each be the topic of a book. In the next chapter, we describe our incredible opportunity to try to control these obstacles.

PRACTITIONER'S NOTE

Dealing with adult issues complicates things for the turn-around team. It is important that the team realize that adults take different approaches to changes that are introduced. The tool kit for chapter 9 includes a cheat sheet that identifies different ways staff can react to change.

THE ROSTER OF PLAYERS

Player Group	Our Staff	Strategies
All Americans		Shared vision, buy-in, and positive leadership. These are marquee players who play vital roles and are known.
Lombardi Award		Need shared vision and positive feedback for their extra efforts. Should be nurtured for leadership.
Cheerleaders		Must focus on playing the game. Must have and be accountable for "game" accomplishments.
Grumblers		May need to be in decision-making loop. Need to get and give positive feedback for successes. May need expectations for where and when grumbling will not be acceptable.
Procrastinators		Need personal plans with time line expectations. May need regular visits and chats about progress to encourage movement.
Chronically and Vocally Overworked		Must have priorities set and be held accountable for reaching those priorities. Need to have regular "reality check" chats with leadership.
Newbies		Need vision sharing and enculturing mentor. Frequent observation with feedback and reshaping also needed.
Keepers of the Flame		Need to focus on what can be not what was. Must commit to vision, have a personal plan for and be held accountable for implementation. May need firm intervention if opposed to change.
Naysayers		Need to be in planning loop. Need specific expectations set for all "vision" talk. May need to be part of success celebrations.
Blockers and Saboteurs		Need strict expectations for cooperation and stated consequences for interference. Need to be moved if a franchise player.

10

A CASE FOR AN ACADEMIC MANAGEMENT ORGANIZATION

Most state accountability systems include sanctions against persistently low-performing schools and districts. In some states, these sanctions include state takeover, whether that means take-over by the state itself or by an outside, third-party group, frequently referred to as an education management organization (EMO). In these cases, control of the school is taken away from the district while turnaround work begins.

Most state accountability systems include sanctions against persistently low-performing schools and districts.

Both options (the state and the EMO) have drawbacks. States may not have the labor power to enter and manage more than a handful of schools; moreover, their assistance teams are typically geared to provide curricular help, not to comprehensively manage the business of running a school. EMOs, while set up to run schools, can be politically polarizing to local constituencies and can create transitioning back problems for schools that were taken out of district programs and systems.

In 2011, we were in a position to bid on assisting a district under considerable pressure to select one of the aforementioned options. The district in question lobbied against both approaches but was adamantly against the idea of the EMO. The state persisted with this option anyway, insisting something drastic be done.

We worked in schools in this district for several years when this took place. Having established professional relationships with the local district leadership, the teachers' union, and the state's regional-assistance team, we knew these schools fairly well. In our opinion, they were not broken so much that a total takeover was necessary. They were well run and for the most part, safe, orderly, and generously staffed. For several years, the district housed a turnaround office in charge of working with its low-performing schools. These persistently low-performing schools also received help and oversight by the state regional-assistance team.

However, the schools still suffered from continually low state test scores. It was our opinion they were low performing for the following three reasons:

1. Instructional priorities were centrally determined and unlinked to any local, causally determined student need. The district efforts to support that curriculum focused on adult issues with its implementation, not on student efficacy or results.

2. The schools themselves were micromanaged and tied to a results and information system that forced them to react to problems identified by untrustworthy, old, or poorly interpreted data. They had little time to take the proactive, causal approach we described in this book.

3. There was a strong compliance culture governing the instructional programs and management of the school. Out-of-the-box thinking was discouraged.

In a nutshell, these schools were stuck in a "doing things right" scenario. Their considerable efforts and energies were directed at doing what they were told to do. However, much of what they were told to do was uninformed by the schoolwork students were producing. Few thought to include the student in the equation.

When the state sent out a request for a proposal for the EMO, we applied. Because we did not see the need for these schools to be taken over totally, we offered a model dealing strictly with teaching and learning. (In this case, we defined ourselves as an academic management organization, or AMO.)

Our proposal outlined ways we would assume responsibility for the instructional management of the schools. This included control over strategic planning and implementation, curriculum, methods, results monitoring and data systems, and instructional support and coaching. We viewed this as an opportunity to implement our approach in its entirety and with some autonomy. Our goal was to manage the academic program until the schools turned around and then phase out our services as we built capacity in the school leadership and faculty.

We saw two components of our proposal as key. First, we enjoyed a direct line to the superintendent's office, bypassing all other district levels. Second, we maintained a collaborative working relationship with the state-assistance team. The line to the superintendent greatly increased the responsiveness of several key units in the hierarchy and gave us control over which supports and services would go into those schools. The collaborative relationship with the state doubled our capacity to deliver services; it helped us navigate state regulations.

The AMO approach was accepted, and we were selected to do the work. The local school board was happy to maintain a degree of control over these schools, as they were still seen by the public as *the district's schools*. The state had an external partner with whom it could align its efforts, and both parties had someone to blame if it didn't work out.

Even though we were unable to start until after school opened, we helped the schools achieve some significant results. There is far more than we can discuss in a single chapter, but our efforts can be summarized as involving the following:

- Through collaboration, we identified priority needs in each school, using Ed Directions' causal analysis of data, student work, and staff capacity.

- As the AMO, we encouraged school staffs to own and address these needs creatively and autonomously.

- We encouraged principals to think out of the box (insisting sometimes) and to adopt a mission-driven approach to leadership.

- We monitored student work and progress in these priority areas and made adjustments in staffing, methods, schedules, and tactics as needed.

- We coordinated the superb coaching support provided by the state-assistance team and district coaches.

- Ed Directions staff members were in the schools enough days to ensure impact.

All seven of the schools reached their score goals on that year's test. The average score gain was more than 80 points (on an 800-point scale), and their reading scores went up by almost 50 percent.

Even though we were unable to start until after school opened, we helped the schools achieve some significant results.

THE READING EXAMPLE

Our academic assistance focused on math, science, writing, and reading. While we do not have time to detail what happened in every area, we will use the area of reading to give you an idea of how the AMO work played out. The reading scores in the high schools were historically quite low with proficiency ranging from single-digit percentages to the teens.

When we came on the scene as the AMO, the district was transitioning from a computer-based curriculum to a text/novel/great books curriculum for these classes. We discovered that the transition was problematic, with little to no professional development helping it, and that materials arrived well after school opened. In addition, many of these teachers were able to follow scripted plans until then, but they were not used to developing lesson plans that could differentiate instruction for different students.

As we began to look deeper into the implementation of the courses, we found several serious issues that helped explain why these low scores were intractable. We found that large numbers of those *dysfluent* students proved fluent in other measures of oral fluency. (The state allowed such evidence to be used to avoid placement in the remedial class.) As we began our probe for causes, we discovered several other factors that needed to be explored in more depth:

- Large numbers of low-scoring students had higher scores in their test history.

- The required remedial reading course enrolled more than two-thirds of the school's freshmen and sophomores.

- Students could only receive elective credit in the remedial course — elective credit they did not need.

- The remedial classes were mainly taught by alternatively certified staff who were laid off from other subject matter areas such as business or electives.

- Students reported to us that they didn't take the test seriously at first because they knew they would be able to retake it several times (proficiency was required for a diploma).

- Students were placed in these courses with little or no screening other than the previous year's test scores.

- The observed levels of student engagement and work in most of these classrooms fell below expectations.

In looking at the reading issues of students enrolled in these classes, we discovered significant numbers of students who could read and understand text at the level of the test but who still scored low on the test itself. We interviewed many of them and had them read and discuss with us in focus groups. Several specific issues emerged, including the following:

- A slow rate of reading prevented many students from completing the test.

- Many students had significant problems with vocabulary.

- Students reported low stamina and failure to commit to struggling with the text, particularly within an unfamiliar or difficult genre.

- Students' question-answering strategies were ineffective, and they frequently used guesswork to choose their answers.

- There were significant attitude and motivation issues related to reading in general and the demands of academic literacy in particular.

- Students resented being in the remedial course.

- Most students (especially males) did not see reading as a significant part of their lives.

- Most students felt they could get by in school without having to do much reading.

We found that large numbers of those dysfluent students proved fluent in other measures of oral fluency.

The more we probed and worked with students, the more we became convinced that the persistently low scores were due more to problems of *aliteracy*, not *illiteracy*. In the past, previous interventions were designed to address the latter, not the former.

We met with the principals to lay out the problems they could most easily and effectively address:

- A large number of students in remedial reading classes were not there for reading problems. The students could read well enough but for varying reasons chose not to.

- The scheduling of courses sometimes prevented students from earning required credits toward graduation and therefore contributed to lower graduation and progression rates.

- The courses had large numbers of poorly trained, alternatively certified teachers instructing those classes, and each school had a wide range of teacher quality. These put constraints on their budget and scheduling flexibility.

- The district had an ingrained culture of compliance within the remedial reading program. Teachers were expected to do what they were told with what they were given, and principals were instructed to stay the course.

- The word among the students was that they didn't have to sweat the reading test until closer to graduation.

When doing the math, we demonstrated that if there were, say, 500 students taking the test, an increase of 10 percent proficiency meant that only 50 more students needed to pass the test.

THE CULTURE OF ALITERACY MEETS THE CULTURE OF COMPLIANCE

The most telling thing was students hated to read — period. When we observed them in their classes, we noticed most worked very hard to *avoid* reading anything at all, academically or recreationally. Much of the reading they did was oral and round robin. We observed a student could safely pass through the whole day without having to read silently to figure out answers to questions or prompts. The students knew how to get the teachers to tell them what they needed to do their work, a luxury they would not have on the state test.

This was obviously problematic on a number of levels. Academically, students rarely had to employ the sort of reading that was assessed on the state test. Many teachers and students avoided the necessary struggles with text that proficient students are accustomed to; without struggle, reading growth is stunted.

> Teachers were pressured to teach the curriculum and stay with the program, even knowing that, in many cases, this was a doomed effort.

Teachers were pressured to teach the curriculum and stay with the program, even knowing that, in many cases, this was a doomed effort. The principals would be good soldiers and promote the district orthodoxy, do the required data analysis, and encourage their coaches to follow the plan. This resulted in the same outcomes year after year.

So, for years, the district planned on the assumption the low scores were because the students could not read and comprehend sufficiently to pass the test. While that may have been the case for a number of the students, it was not what kept a larger number of them from scoring proficiently.

It was clear to us, then, that what made low reading scores in these schools such an intractable problem was the combination of a broad spectrum of student engagement issues coupled with instructional inputs designed to address the wrong problems. Persistent low scores create major perception problems; they signal to stakeholders that students cannot read well enough to do high school work, which can lead to a "What's the use?" mentality on the part of both adults and students. Kids think they are *dumb*, teachers think the kids don't care (or worse), administrators think teachers cannot teach, and the community has evidence these schools are failures.

THE PLAN

This is what we proposed at the end of that September. (Remember, we did not start until late August). We asked the principals to select their most capable reading teachers and reschedule students based on several metrics. We probed the data and worked with students to see who among them would willingly try a new reading course.

We worked with the state and selected district coaches to develop a curriculum that would get students reading again, engage them with hot topics, create a classroom community of readers, and challenge them to struggle with text at the level of the assessment. We provided customized, targeted professional development for the teachers. These coaches also provided daily support to teachers in the schools and helped with materials and feedback.

Essentially, we treated these new classes as working models and encouraged the schools to use them to coach the successful methods into the other reading classrooms. The teachers we trained became a professional learning community (PLC) and would meet periodically to share successes and struggles. They also became experts in their own buildings, and many gained seats of influence on leadership teams and departments.

Finally, we implemented our own progress-monitoring system that periodically assessed students with checks parallel to the state assessment; we developed an item-analysis method that targeted error evaluation significantly and focused on reteaching.

This whole approach to turning around a school was a dramatic departure from typical business in this district. Soon, teachers reported that they felt more empowered and autonomous, and principals saw evidence of engagement and enthusiasm and reported that these classes were creating a buzz. Students began to read more independently and engage more in the community of readers that many of the classes became.

As the year proceeded, the progress-monitoring system revealed other priority needs. For instance, students had a tremendous tendency to respond impulsively on assessments; guesses were the default response strategy. They showed both an unwillingness and an inability to concentrate for sufficient periods of time, and they struggled to select the best answer when given two plausible ones. These mental habits were schoolwide problems, and the teachers and instructional coaches attempted to address them in a variety of ways. Leadership got involved as well. The schools' academic focus sharpened considerably as a result.

The AMO model only lasted one year. All seven schools exceeded their target scores, and five of the seven came off the state priority list entirely. (The other two just missed the 25 percent reading target required to exit.) We felt the year proved the basic assumptions behind the model: that those closest to the student know the most about student capacity and performance. With coaching and guidance, this *bottom-up* approach to problem-solving can help identify key issues that, when effectively addressed, can move the school. The students and their work can inform what and how we teach better than a set program or curriculum — the students and their teachers know better what they need.

11

CONCLUSIONS: ARE WE THERE YET?

In this book, we described the evolution of our approach to educational leadership, from a focus on managing conventional best practices to a focus on an approach to using multiple data streams to inform decisions about educating learners and performers. Our protocols, data-collection documents, and PD series focus on the process of managing learning and performance, not on managing schools and teachers. We approached teacher improvement and teacher evaluation efforts from the student side noting first what the students have to do, and then, assessing the teacher's ability to empower a student to do that and to grow as a learner and performer. This book reflects that change of perspective and how it impacted the way we do our jobs.

We explained in the first few chapters that as long as we focused our school improvement efforts on only the adult behaviors and looked only at the input side of the question, any gains we made in student performance and scores were very inconsistent. It was not until we started looking at what was expected of students and focusing on what the *students* had to do to reach those expectations that we understood that we were asking the wrong questions and solving the wrong problems.

Trying to approach the output or performance problems from the input side made our efforts accidental in planning for the real student-performance issues. It was only after we concentrated on output expectations and preparing students to meet those expectations that we introduced intentionality to our planning, data collection, progress monitoring, and teacher evaluations. This book reflects not a criticism of what we knew but an evaluation of how we could use that knowledge in a more intentional and student-focused way.

It was only after we concentrated on output expectations and preparing students to meet those expectations that we introduced intentionality to our planning, data collection, progress monitoring, and teacher evaluations.

In subsequent chapters, we described how changes in perspective provided us with the most leverage to affect student academic performance. Perhaps the most critical issue for readers to understand is how to identify what student improvement and *proficiency* mean for students in a given classroom. Our earliest work defined proficiency in terms of a set of content needing to be covered. The narrow definition limited our ability to develop a curriculum capable of strengthening all the capacities students needed to be proficient performers (their ability to demonstrate what they learned in the manner in which they would be assessed). Unpacking the standards and defining proficient learners and performers along five dimensions was a major development in our approach; it gave direction to student-performance expectations and provided a filter for evaluating materials, teaching strategies, data needs, and assessment strategies. Schools that do not unpack standards along all five dimensions (who only unpack to the content level) never develop the holistic approach they need to turn a struggling school around.

When we first got involved in school improvement, we thought data management was the greatest shared strength of our group. We were experts at test report interpretation, disaggregation, and (what we thought was) best-practice data mining. We knew the different test forms and could identify choices for specific areas of reading, math, science, or social studies. What we didn't know was that, like the Platte River, our data management was a mile wide and an inch deep.

We could collect data points telling us the same thing over and over. However, when we tried to plan from those data points, we found none of them told us what we needed to know about student learning and student performance. They did nothing to determine root cause and the point at which student work broke down. The evolution of our data management — from triangulating and disaggregating to data rooms containing purposeful collections of student learning, performance and assessment work — is one of the major pieces contributing to our growth as a company. Many of the schools we have worked with mentioned the modifications we made to their PLC discussions in the data room were the factors that made the greatest difference in their classroom practice.

As with data management, the changes we made in our progress monitoring changed the way we did business as a support group. In the beginning, we tracked changes in input. *Were the teachers providing more thinking work? Were they asking high-level questions?* As long as our attention was focused on inputs, we could monitor changes in the input but not in the output. Once we defined the output and used that as a distinct goal for all students, we ensured all student and teacher work moved every student in the right direction. We could be intentional about what we wanted both teachers and students to do.

This led us to what we call progress monitoring: implementation and impact-monitoring programs. Now we look at the quality of implementation to make sure all students are engaged in activities that will enable them to move toward our established goals, and then we evaluate the impact that the strategy has on performance to see if the results are consistent with our goals. If they are not, we evaluate the input to see what should be done differently for all students to reach the goals. The progress-monitoring piece was considered valuable by most of the schools we assisted. Many of them pointed out that by focusing on implementation and impact, we could establish the link between teacher work, student work, and student performance. They felt this forced them to become more intentional in the way they designed lessons, monitored for learning, and developed support systems for teachers and students.

Not all aspects of our work were so readily accepted. The issue of best practice (when it is not situationally best practice) was the one most difficult for schools to understand. We accepted "traditional" best practice is not *always* best practice irrespective of context; conditional and situational best practice was a difficult paradigm shift for our group and for schools. It was one of the issues creating barriers with central office staff, other vendors, and teachers who had been trained and identified as masters of a strategy or technique.

One special education teacher challenged us in a workshop: "What you're saying is that since my students are all over the spectrum in terms of needs and abilities, I'm going to have to find appropriate practice for each one of them?" Yes, that was what we were saying. If we do not identify what students must do and what needs to happen to make sure they can do it, we will always have underperforming schools, underperforming students, and performance gaps. As long as our best practices are best practices for some and not for all, we cannot avoid having some students left out of optimal learning environments. This challenge doesn't seem so daunting if we keep traditional wisdom and input-focused institutions from getting in the way of our development of best-practice classrooms.

If we do not identify what students must do and what needs to happen to make sure they can do it, we will always have underperforming schools, underperforming students, and performance gaps.

When we discussed other obstacles in our turnaround work, we chose to focus on those we thought were most significant. For several of us, the highest-leverage area we had to conquer was the commitment to an orthodoxy that mandated effective management of adults and resources and only gave lip service to outcome-based instructional leadership. We found people did not want to stop doing things they thought worked for students even if those things only worked for a few of the students or the data showed the intervention to be only somewhat effective. Getting movement from that mindset to one emphasizing performance gains for everybody was tough when it got educators out of their comfort zones or go-to practitioner skill sets; schools being expected to move everybody at least to the level of their potential proved to require a major effort in many schools. Other barriers are linked to this particular problem; conflicting initiatives, compliance cultures, and turf battles are a result of people having a commitment to an orthodoxy inconsistent with what teachers in the classrooms need to do to move the students from where they are to where they need to be.

Finally, we included a chapter on the AMO model we developed for historically low-performing schools. This model allowed us to help bring tighter focus on student needs and performance expectations. With the AMO's direct link to the superintendent, we avoided turf battles, insulated the schools from conflicting initiatives, and controlled the PD to the extent that it represented what the teachers needed to know to make all their students learners and proficient performers. We defined PD as more than just training — we included training, of course, but it also became planning, monitoring, and adjustment time; observation and feedback time; and PLC discussion time.

With the AMO team in the building on a regular basis, we reshaped the way classrooms operated and the way adults looked at classrooms. We conducted observations of student engagement and the level of student work as well as the quality of the work the teacher was doing. Most of our schools developed portfolios of learning, performance, and testing work; however, we were not able to overcome all the barriers that can exist in schools. For example, in some schools, tardiness remained a problem throughout the year, but we overcame most of the high-leverage barriers and we experienced positive results.

The thinking behind this book was to share with you some of the things we, as an organization, learned about improving student performance. We realize that in terms of ensuring proficient performance from all students and turning around turnaround schools, we still have a long way to go. While we continue to grow as a learning organization, we see even bigger game changers on the horizon that excite us very much.

PRACTITIONER'S NOTE

Once you complete *Turning Around Turnaround Schools*, the authors suggest you retake the initial self-study at the beginning of the book and reach your own conclusions.

CASE STUDIES

DATA-DRIVEN INSTRUCTION: OUR JOURNEY FROM DATA WALLS TO ACTIONABLE DATA

Yvonne Rambo, Director of Turnaround Schools, Indianapolis Public Schools

Through our work with Frank DeSensi in the late 1990s and early 2000s, we were made aware of the critical importance of using data to *drive instruction*. In the beginning, we filled binders and data rooms with colorful charts. Red, yellow, and green graphs covered our walls, separated by assessment category. We discovered that this awareness level of student-achievement data sets was only the beginning for us, that we would soon need more individualized, comprehensive tools to effectively discuss and plan using these data sets.

As we introduced the data to teachers, it was evident to us that they needed to be broken down by student. We also discovered that we needed to have data on more than just assessments; we needed attendance data, discipline data, teacher attendance and evaluation data, mobility data, subgroup categories, reading Lexiles, and enrollment data. At this phase of our journey, the data became real, specific, and individualized.

Then, we developed Data Rooms 2.0 because the teachers needed more and better data to make an instructional change for their students. We changed the way we set up the data rooms — changing, for example, from lots of charts to individualized student data cards. Each student's card included his or her complete academic bio: subgroups, reading levels, and so on. We painted our walls in stoplight colors and placed students' data cards on the walls according to their results in the latest high-stakes assessments. This visual depiction of students and their trend data made us more effective. We noticed more. For example, on certain assessments, we found that the majority of our ESL students were failing or thriving, and we saw other significant issues we hadn't noticed before. Teachers would physically move their students' data cards from one color to the next and have meaningful conversations about what to do next to support them.

Data 3.0 now emphasizes students owning (aggregating and tracking) their data. We have created data résumés for our students with data goals and action steps. We have also scripted teacher-student data talks with action planning as the end result. One of the most exciting elements of Data Rooms 3.0 is the *Monster Roster*, a document showing all the students' data on one sheet with an intervention column added. During our data talks, we discuss each student and assign interventions from our newly developed intervention menus. This Monster Roster is a tool that we have used to ensure that every student receives the support and enrichment that he or she needs to be successful.

GETTING THE WHOLE LEARNING ORGANIZATION ON THE BUS

Butch Martin, Educational Coach and Retired Principal

In our circles, the phrase caught on sometime around the year 2000: "We have to get everyone at this school on the bus." We must believe in and live up to our mission statements. We must become a team and start to foster a greater collaboration, so that we can improve.

No one is saying this was wrong. Schools need to do those things. I think it is important to *make sure everyone's on the bus* — but direction and planning matter. If just having consensus is as far as we think, the folks could be on the wrong bus headed in the wrong direction.

When we hire the bright, energetic, motivated teachers we want to work in urban schools, the first thing that has to happen to them is retraining. They have to be retrained because they will not understand the difference between the input and output models. In fact, they may have never heard of the terminology.

If they have never heard of the input model, that's beneficial for the trainer. Instead of undoing something not working, we can focus their attention on something that will work.

The input model is teacher-driven and teacher-focused, while the output model is focused on student work and what the student is doing. In the output model, the teacher is comparing the student's work to proficient work as defined by the state. When the work is compared, the teacher will find the gaps or deficits. Instruction begins at this point because the teacher has to work with the student to eliminate the deficits through intentional work sessions. The teacher becomes the coach: The teacher has to coach the student just as a football or basketball coach works with players to maximize their performance for the game.

We have been successful getting this point of student-focused design versus teacher-focused design across to the teachers and principals. Some pick it up quickly and have very few problems making the transition. With others, it takes a little time, and they have to watch colleagues or even be teamed with a partner. But they do get there.

The toughest group to change is the group that sits between the principals and the superintendents — the central office personnel. People in testing, curriculum, and instruction; professional development; and ECE have heart attacks with this new approach, even though we can present them with improved results. They get really upset when new methods establish our credibility with the teachers and principals. When the folks at the school level start to ignore the central office staff, then our days in the district start counting down.

We may have the superintendent *on the bus*. We may have the teachers and principals *on the bus*. Then, when kids see and feel improvement, they also get on the bus. The two groups that are usually left out are the central office folks and the school board. This is a major problem — we need to be proactive with these two groups, so they get the same information the teachers and principals receive. They need to be part of the team bailing water *out* of the boat instead of dumping water in. They need to see where they can assist. However, we need to get it across that we are not after their jobs.

In the future, we don't think it's going to be good enough to have only the superintendent, principals, and teachers on board. School board members and central office staff must have a seat on the bus. If they are riding the same bus, they will all be heading in the same direction together.

APPENDIX

TOOL-KIT KEY

Chapter	Tool	Description
Before/After Reading Book	Initial School Self-Study	Individuals or PLC groups can use this prior to reading the book to help initiate self-assessment and reflection. It can also be used as a prereading or post-reading tool for identifying changed attitudes. The self-study tests educators' perceptions of prioritizing and planning in a school improvement environment.
1	Red-Flag Analysis Set	Provide guidelines and a flowchart for doing a red-flag analysis of state assessment report documents. This set helps educators identify patterns and discontinuities between and among test scores; this can also lead to a data mining experience that changes the way they look at planning to improve their students.
	Doing the Math Worksheet	Provides a structure for mining test scores to identify red-flag areas of concern, set goals for this year's assessment cycle, and quantify those goals in terms of current student numbers. Doing the math enables educators to determine current status of the school and identify groups of students that must be moved for the school to reach its goal.

Chapter	Tool	Description
1 (cont.)	Test Format Mastery Worksheet	The worksheet used by teachers to identify test question types that the students have and have not mastered to enable targeted-assistance groups. The test format mastery gives educators a tool for monitoring student mastery of the different types of questions they will face on the state assessment.
2	Unpacking a Standard/ Planning Set	Includes three of the worksheets ED uses to walk schools through the standards-based curriculum development process, moving from unpacking the expectations of the standard through the development of units, and lessons to deliver the learnings identified.
	The Five-Legged Model Support Materials	The five-legged model materials are used to introduce a staff to the competency areas that support student performance on assessment.
3	Competency Worksheet for the Five-Legged Model and the Transition Competencies	The competency worksheet looks at both the five-legged model and the transition competencies and encourages staff to plan to build competencies that are missing.
	Point of Breakdown Worksheet with a Planning Chart	The point of breakdown worksheet helps school leaders identify the point at which student work breaks down and then begins remediating the students work at that point by addressing the identified cause.
4	Causal Checklist	This is a page from the student profile ED collects on students to help determine priority need and group students by priority need. The causal checklist identifies cognitive and noncognitive indicators that can have positive or negative effects on student performance.
	Independence Log	The independence log identifies the students comfort zone of independence and identifies students to become more independent before the time of the test.

Chapter	Tool	Description
4 (cont.)	Readiness Checklist	A worksheet used by teachers to assess student readiness to do grade-level learning and assessing work. The readiness checklist identifies the student characteristics connected with success in school.
	Student as Learner Checklist	A worksheet used by teachers to assess student proficiency as learners and identify areas of the learning process the students need to develop more fully in the formative period. The learner checklist identifies characteristics connected to effective learning.
	Student as Performer Checklist	A worksheet used by teachers to evaluate the student as a performer and identify areas of the performing process the student needs to develop more fully in the formative period. These checklists help identify the pattern of student strengths and weaknesses that they take to classroom and assessment work.
5	Classroom Observation Tool	A worksheet used by school leaders to observe student and teacher interaction in the opening and formative periods of the academic year. It has a focus on the nature and quality of student work assigned and student engagement in network and academic rituals and routines used in the class.
	Student Work Analysis	A worksheet used by teachers to analyze the student as a worker and producer of learning work. The student work analysis allows teachers to do a diagnostic analysis of a student product.
	Teacher Work Analysis	This worksheet can be used by teachers for self-study or by administrators for guiding PLC discussions of teacher planning and delivery of lessons. It focuses on teaching with the end in mind and engaging students in effective learning work. Teacher work analysis enables school leaders and teachers to do a diagnostic analysis of a teacher's lesson plan.

Chapter	Tool	Description
5 (cont.)	Data Management Self-Study	Ed Directions has several systems checklists. This checklist focuses on the school's data management system and helps schools identify gaps in their data management plan. The data management self-study gives school leadership a chance to compare their data strategies against what's considered a best practice in data management systems.
6	School Plan Enabling Checklist	This checklist is used as a part of ED's strategic planning module. It identifies elements that must be included in a plan for a plan to work as advertised. It gives schools a chance to revise their plan to include all the elements needed for success.
	Planning Self-Assessment	This is another systems check, this time focusing on planning (strategic, logistic, and tactical). The self-assessment again gives school leadership a chance to compare its planning process against what is considered best practice planning.
	Teacher Tactical Plan and Translation Activity	One of the things we have found that schools rarely did was have teachers take the school strategic plan and turn it into their own personal action plan. This tool guides teachers through the development of an action plan and can be used by administrators for PLC and evaluation discussions.
	Systems Self-Assessment for Planning	This is another systems check, this time focusing on planning (strategic, logistic, and tactical). The self-assessment again gives school leadership a chance to compare its planning process against what is considered best practice planning.

Chapter	Tool	Description
7	Academic Rituals and Routines Checklist	This summary sheet is used by teachers to check their use of effective academic and learning rituals and routines. It includes the minimum list of learning rituals and routines expected in a standards-based classroom. The checklist identifies academic rituals and routines that, if taught and mastered by students in the first three weeks of school, can have a major impact on student success.
	Instructional Self-Assessment	Another systems check focusing on developing students who can perform at expected levels. It deals with both curriculum development and curriculum delivery.
8	Academic Review Debriefing Tool	At the end of each academic review, ED conducts a debriefing session on the academic review and encourages schools to agree or disagree with the findings and recommendations and use their discussion as a starting point for a new strategic plan. The debriefing tool helps schools identify red flag areas and prioritize the areas they wish to change.
9	Roster of Players Worksheet	A change agent needs to know how participants will react to change. The roster of players identifies different responses to change and how those responses impact the change process.

ACKNOWLEDGMENTS

Joe, Frank and Robert would like to express our heartfelt gratitude to all those who helped make this second edition possible. Our colleagues, partners, mentors and mentees, as well as the schools and districts with which we worked, all played a part in both the evolution of our approach to education (and specifically our approach to turnaround schools) and the actual content of this book. Their feedback and suggestions about tools and additional insights they sought were critical to making the second edition more practical and user friendly for educational practitioners.

In particular, we would like to thank our copy and line editors: Bob Johnson, Susan Draus, Hilary Jastram, and Kate Colbert. Our writing mentor, Cathy Fyock (author of *On Your Mark*), was instrumental in defining the book's scope and voice and helping to organize the content. We would also like to thank Iam Bennett for lending his artistic talents to the cover design and interior graphics, and Kate Colbert and Courtney Hudson at Silver Tree Publishing for seeing the value in the second edition and for bringing this book to market.

And while we can not list them all by name, we would like to thank all of Educational Directions' leadership coaches, content coaches, data coaches, project managers, administrators, marketers, and support staff. They all played a part in making this a success. This book is the product of the important work we do every day.

INFLUENCES

While this book does not use the specific research of other authors, we still need to acknowledge some of the important influences in the development of our approach and biases.

Philip Schlechty came to Louisville, Kentucky, in the early 1980s to direct the Gheens Center for Jefferson County Public Schools. His vision of the school culture, which defined students and not adults as the workers, opened the way for us to approach school leadership and change through the work of the student. Our focus on outputs is in many respects indebted to him. He influenced us greatly.

Michael Fullan's and Andy Hargreaves's research and writing on organizational change in school cultures taught us that the barriers to change were based in certain social and political realities of human interaction — and that common sense really is a useful best practice.

We also must mention Linda Darling-Hammond and her leadership in making the student the center of change efforts. Her optimism helped energize those of us who work in this field. To wit, we must mention the important influences of Ted Sizer, Sarason Seymour, Diane Ravitch, Ann Lieberman, and many others.

Richard Elmore's influence of late was especially important. He reaffirms that meaningful school improvement can only be effectively approached through the linking of the curriculum, the teacher, and the learner; improvement in any one must be balanced by corresponding improvement in the other two.

In the area of academic literacy, we have recently been greatly guided by the writings and research of Tim Shanahan. He gives excellent guidance to any educator wrestling with the literacy demands of the Common Core State Standards.

The important ethnographic work of Shirley Brice Heath continues to inform our awareness of sociolinguistic factors that frequently arise in turnaround work. We have also learned a great deal from the work of Gloria Ladson-Billings. Her book *The Dreamkeepers: Successful Teachers of African American Children* (John Wiley & Sons, 2013) remains a touchstone text for us, as does Alfred Tatum's *Teaching Reading to Black Adolescent Males: Closing the Achievement Gap* (Stenhouse Publishers, 2005). We also want to cite Doreen Kimura and Michael Gurian for their contributions to the effects of gender differences on learning.

Our approach to the development of critical thinking and metacognition in children was shaped in large part by the work of Robert Marzano, Richard Paul, Barry Beyer, and Arthur Costa. Lately, we have been exploring the exciting new developments in brain research and cognition in the works of David Sousa, Robin Fogarty, Renate and Jeffrey Caine, and J. David Cresswell.

One of the authors, Robert Knight, needs to acknowledge the professional growth he experienced from his tenure with the National Center on Education and the Economy/America's Choice. The organization, created by Marc Tucker and Judy Codding (aided mightily by Peter Hill and others too numerous to mention), came as close to perfection as a professional learning community can come.

Finally, there are more Kentucky educators than we could possibly name who deserve mention. What we learned from them, with them, and even despite some of them during the initial years of the Kentucky Education Reform Act molded our core knowledge base. It was a heady time for those of us involved in its implementation and an opportunity for which we are extremely grateful.

ABOUT THE AUTHORS

FRANK DESENSI

Frank DeSensi is the founder of Educational Directions, LLC, which consults with schools and school districts in the southeastern and midwestern United States. A retired educator, Frank spent 35 years in a variety of teaching and administrative positions. He taught at the university, college, secondary, and middle-school levels; worked in the central office as a curriculum specialist; and held both principal and assistant principal positions. From 1993 to 1998, Frank served as a Kentucky Distinguished Educator, helping to turn around schools that were labeled *in decline* or *in crisis* under the provisions of the Kentucky Education Reform Act. Frank helped develop the STAR training program for new DEs and served as a trainer in the Kentucky Leadership Academy. He jointly holds patents for three data-management systems for schools.

ROBERT KNIGHT, EDD

Robert Knight is the director of literacy for Educational Directions. He spent 40 years in public education as a teacher, literacy and leadership specialist, principal, and change agent. After a 27-year career with Jefferson County Public Schools and the Kentucky Department of Education, he worked with the National Center on Education and the Economy/America's Choice and Transformations by Design and is currently a senior consultant for Educational Directions. Dr. Knight's work took him to more than a dozen states and 75 schools.

JOE DESENSI, EDD

Joe DeSensi is the president of Educational Directions. He has an undergraduate degree from Bellarmine University, a graduate degree in computer-resource management from Webster University, and a doctorate in leadership education from Spalding University. Dr. DeSensi has worked with Fortune 500 companies, federal and local government, and school districts across the Southeast. He developed custom and enterprise software to help districts track data and target students' needs, and he holds patents in school data-management software and database integration. Dr. DeSensi also teaches graduate classes in leadership, ethics, and operational design at Spalding University.

Made in the USA
Columbia, SC
13 February 2019